HOW THE WORLD BEGAN:

CREATION
IN MYTHS & LEGENDS

GILLY CAMERON COOPER
Illustrations by Patricia Ludlow

southwater

This edition is published by Southwater

Southwater is an imprint of Anness Publishing Ltd
Hermes House, 88–89 Blackfriars Road, London SE1 8HA
tel. 020 7401 2077; fax 020 7633 9499
www.southwaterbooks.com; info@anness.com

© Anness Publishing Ltd 2003, 2006

UK agent: The Manning Partnership Ltd,
6 The Old Dairy, Melcombe Road,
Bath BA2 3LR; tel. 01225 478444; fax 01225 478440;
sales@manning-partnership.co.uk

UK distributor: Grantham Book Services Ltd, Isaac Newton Way,
Alma Park Industrial Estate, Grantham, Lincs NG31 9SD;
tel. 01476 541080; fax 01476 541061; orders@gbs.tbs-ltd.co.uk

North American agent/distributor: National Book Network,
4501 Forbes Boulevard, Suite 200, Lanham, MD 20706;
tel. 301 459 3366; fax 301 429 5746; www.nbnbooks.com

Australian agent/distributor: Pan Macmillan Australia, Level 18,
St Martins Tower, 31 Market St, Sydney, NSW 2000;
tel. 1300 135 113; fax 1300 135 103; customer.service@macmillan.com.au

New Zealand agent/distributor: David Bateman Ltd,
30 Tarndale Grove, Off Bush Road, Albany, Auckland;
tel. (09) 415 7664; fax (09) 415 8892

A CIP catalogue record for this book is available from the British Library.

Publisher: Joanna Lorenz
Managing Editor: Linda Fraser
Editors: Rebecca Clunes and Joy Wotton
Map Artwork: David Cook
Picture Research: Su Alexander
Copy Editor: Tracey Kelly
Consultant: Michael Jordan

Previously published as *Myths and Legends from Around the World: How
The World Began*

10 9 8 7 6 5 4 3 2 1

Picture credits
b=bottom, t=top, r=right, l=left, m=middle
The Publishers wish to thank the following for permission to
reproduce illustrations. Corbis/Raymond Gehman: 8b, /Dean Conger:
38b, /Neil Rabinowitz: 42b. Peter Newark's American Pictures: 11b.
Oxford Scientific Films/Michael Fogden: 13br, /Peter Ryley: 14b, /Steve
Turner: 45b. Michael Culler: 18b. Nature Picture Library/Anup Shah: 20b.
The Art Archive/Egyptian Museum Cairo/Dagli Orti: 25b. Werner Forman
Archive/National Palace Museum Taipei: 33b. ImageState: 36m

Contents

Before Time Began

"Why am I? How did the world come to be? Was there nothing before there was anything? How did nothing turn into something?"

Since the beginning of time, people have asked questions like these. Before they had even learned to write, early humans wondered how their world began. They could understand the simple tasks of hunting, or foraging for food, of survival. But why did night follow day (or was it the other way around)? And who made the stars, the seas, rivers and mountains, plants and animals?

Was a thunderstorm or a sudden strike of lightning a sign or warning from another world? Myths and rituals, gods, and spirits helped early people to explain such mysteries.

How myths came to be

All over the world, as people gathered in families, tribes, and communities, they invented different solutions to the mystery of existence. Our knowledge today has piled up from centuries of discovery, the work of scientists through the ages, and from exploring Space. Early humans pieced together their own observations and understandings of the world with stories of past times that had been handed down. Slowly, stories took shape that helped explain how and why the world and everything in it came to be, and these stories became part of a people's traditions, beliefs, and culture. Some stories were spoken; others took the form of chants, songs, and dances, or were carved into sculptures, or painted on the walls of caves. Mythologies developed as the stories were passed down through the generations by families, medicine men, and priests.

So which version is right?

You may have figured out some answers for yourself on how the world began, with the help of information gathered from your parents and teachers, from religious books, such as the Bible or the Koran, and from reading about scientific discoveries. You probably have friends from other cultures and religions who have completely different ideas. Scientists tell us that animals, including humans, formed over

Some ancient stories were transcribed on to clay tablets, and later discovered by modern archaeologists. Many of these stones have been translated, so that we now know more about the ancient world.

aeons of time from more and more complex arrangements of cells. This doesn't necessarily make creation myths a lot of nonsense, or some beliefs true and others false. They are just different ways of describing the beginning of life on Earth in symbols that people from very different cultures could understand in the context of their own lives and knowledge.

The lotus flower features in myths from Egypt and India—both countries where ancient civilizations developed in rich river valleys. When the lotus came into bloom, it was a sign that spring had arrived. The flower became a symbol of new growth and fertility.

Dead or alive?

The myths of civilizations that are long gone, such as those of ancient Greece, Egypt, and Mesopotamia, may no longer be believed, but they are enjoyed as rich and interesting stories. They give an insight into how people of ancient times thought and lived. Many myths, though, are living beliefs. Jewish, Christian and Muslim people believe that one god created the heavens and Earth and all the creatures on it. The aborigines of Australia believe in many creator Ancestors, whose living spirits are still in the places, plants, and creatures around them today. What every creation myth has in common, though, is a belief in superhuman power or powers that got things going in the first place.

How things change!

Even myths from the same part of the world exist in many different versions. Have you ever played the party game in which one person whispers a sentence to another, who then whispers it to the next person, and so on? By the time the last person announces what he or she has heard, the sentence has often changed quite a lot from the original! Myths are a little like this. Stories were passed on from generation to generation—like the game of Chinese Whispers—but on the way, they changed, or new versions appeared. Tribes and communities grew, fragmented, and spread. Aboriginal peoples spread all over the Australian continent, splitting into thousands of separate tribes as they moved across the land. Each tribe added its own characters and adventures to the ancestral creation story. Just as scientists constantly rework and revise truths and discoveries made by earlier thinkers and scholars, so people adjusted the age-old stories to fit in with newfound knowledge and changing lifestyles.

Many peoples migrated great distances in search of more space or more fertile land. They clashed with other tribes and sometimes conquered them. In this way, separate and often quite different cultures merged, and ancestral stories got mixed up with each other. New experiences, characters, landscapes, and

The Creation in the Jewish and Christian scriptures is masterminded by one God. Many creation myths tell of a single superhuman power or powers that triggered the world into being.

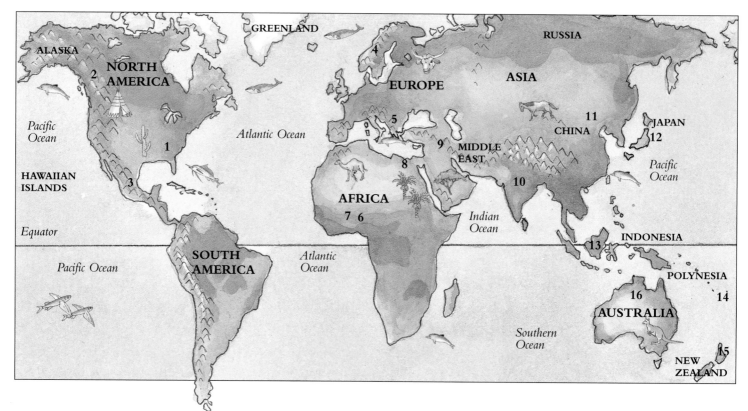

When these Japanese creator gods met around the Heavenly Pillar, the man had to speak first. Myths often have clues as to what is considered proper behavior.

lifestyles were absorbed. Scandinavian myths describe a land of heat lying far to the south of the frozen northern land, and of gods battling for power. This echoes the migration of German peoples from warmer climates in eastern Asia to icy Scandinavian lands in the north, and the many conflicts they must have had with tribes they encountered on the way. Powerful conquerors often rewrote traditional stories to boost their reputations, by adding their own conquests and the glorious exploits of their ancestors. Chinese and Japanese myths were adapted by successive dynasties. They were even used as a means of propaganda, to put the people they ruled in their place, and to show them how to behave.

Myths from around the world

The map shows where the stories in this book come from.
1. The Master of Breath (North America)
2. Old Man's Magic (North America)
3. Five Aztec Worlds (Central America)
4. Land of Ice (Northern Europe)
5. Order from Chaos (Greece)
6. The Evil Thorn Tree (West Africa)
7. Obtalala and the Hen (West Africa)
8. Birth from Water (Egypt)
9. Marduk and the Tablets of Destiny (Middle East)
10. Gods and Lotus Flowers (India)
11. The Giant Who Made the World (China)
12. Trials of Love (Japan)
13. Animal Magic (Indonesia)
14. The Cosmic Coconut (Polynesia)
15. Violent Beginnings (New Zealand)
16. Dreaming (Australia)

Reading and enjoying

Many of the stories may seem strange at first, for they are about alien worlds of long ago, when people lived and thought very differently. If something doesn't seem to make sense to you because it does not fit in with your own knowledge or lifestyle, suspend your disbelief—just as you do in a fantasy adventure story with gigantic wizards and magical potions. Picture the world of the peoples who created the myths. Imagine the Aztec jungle with snakes slithering in the dense undergrowth and the iridescent plumes of the quetzal bird flashing through the trees— and you will recognize the plumed serpent god Quetzalcoatl. The children of a tribe would have heard the stories many times as they sat around a camp fire. As you read and reread these stories, you will be drawn more and more into their worlds and their magic. If you then tell your friends about them, you will be keeping the traditional tales alive.

Strange ideas

In the world of mythology, planets such as the Earth, sun and moon, elements such as the rain and wind, and even conditions such as love and death are often thought of as gods. This can be confusing at first, so when this occurs in this book, the words are shown as proper names with a capital letter at the beginning, as in the Greek

Nyx, the Greek goddess of night, gave birth to daylight. In myths, planets and elements are what they are, and they are also gods.

god Chaos. Soon, you will accept that an ocean can be a god as well as an ocean, and that winds and forests have human feelings!

The names of some of the gods and spirits are unfamiliar, too, and many of them look completely unpronounceable. Try copying them down, syllable by syllable, and then read them slowly, enjoying their sounds. You will discover that some of the names sound like the things they represent. The word "Shu"—say it out loud—for example, is the ancient Egyptian god of air.

Making connections

Soak up the mystery of myths and you will make some astonishing discoveries. Among all the wildly different versions of how the world began, you will gradually pick up common threads of human thought running through them all. Many creation myths tell stories about swirling matter and chaos, and forces of power waiting to be unleashed. Some people believed there was a primal god or spirit who brought life into being at the beginning of all things.

Before time began, say the Bambara people of West Africa, there was only silence. Myths from many parts of the world say that, at the very beginning, there was total silence. Some peoples, including both the ancient Egyptians and the Chinese, believed life began with a cosmic breath.

Another common theme is that of a great explosion caused by the collision of opposing forces, so releasing life-giving energy. Such an idea is not so very different from how today's scientists think the world began. The Big Bang theory describes how the explosion of dense matter marked the beginning of our universe. When you start seeing such connections, you will find that these ancient stories often do not seem quite as strange as they do on first reading.

Today's Big Bang theory describes how a ball of intense heat and density exploded and triggered the Universe into being. Many myths offer similar theories of chaos, darkness, swirling matter, and sudden energy.

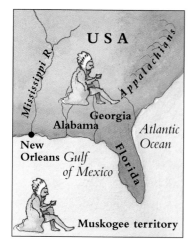

The Master of Breath

The ancestors of the Muskogees, or Creek Indians, from southeastern North America, lived near rivers that cut through the primeval forest. They fished in rivers and lakes, and reaped seasonal supplies of fruits, nuts, and game. Gradually, they learned to sow and harvest plants, and settled in the river valleys. Their myths reflect the special bond they believe exists between humans and the natural world.

The silent mound of earth rose black and solid against the glistening, star-studded night. It had been raised in a time long ago, by the distant ancestors of the Muskogee people, as a burial mound for their brave warriors. For the men, women, and children, grandparents and young men and women alike, the earth island was a place of safety, where they felt close to their gods. It was a symbol of their deep link with the land around them.

"How do you think we came to be?" the tribal elder asked, as he began his story. "For before time began, there were no mountains and plains, no trees or running rivers, only an ocean that stretched for ever and ever, in all directions.

"There were, though, two creatures, a pair of pigeons," the elder continued. "The birds flew back and forth over the vast ocean, seeing nothing but gleaming, featureless water.

"Then, one day, they stopped during midflight. They watched in astonishment as a green blade cut through the waves, followed by another, and then another. It was grass, just like the grass in our fields."

The eyes of the gathered crowd followed the elder's gaze as it turned to fall on the dark mound behind him. "The Earth grew into a planet, and right in its center, there was a high, steep hill. This island hill was Nunne Chaha. It was to be the home of the god Esaugetuh Emissee."

The pigeons find grass growing through the waters.

The breath of life

The tribal elder stopped for a moment. "Children," he said, "let's all say that name."

The children spoke the name "Esaugetuh Emissee." It sounded like the sigh of a breeze in the trees, a gentle wave of life-giving breath.

"That is just how it is supposed to sound," explained the elder. "For Esaugetuh Emissee is god of the life-giving air, ruler of the winds, the Master of Breath."

CONNECTIONS

• The Muskogees are also known today as the Creek Indians, a name given to them by European settlers. The tribes lived along the banks of creeks—sheltered branches of the big rivers.

• The Creeks were a branch of the ancient Mississippian peoples, who settled in the southeastern part of North America, where the state of Georgia is today. The Mississippian Culture was at its peak from AD 800 to the early 1700s.

• The skills that Esaugetuh Emissee taught were used by the Indians throughout their history. It is said that their women were the first farmers of North America.

This grass-covered burial mound in Cartersville, Georgia, was built for warriors by Etowah Indians, ancestors of the Muskogees. The tribal priest lived in a temple on top. When he died, the temple was destroyed and a new temple was built for his successor.

The Master of Breath, Esaugetuh Emissee, breathes life into the small clay figures he has made. That is how the first Muskogee people came to be.

He continued the story.

"One day, as Esaugetuh Emissee was sitting on his hill, gazing over the oceans stretching around him, he idly picked up some soft clay. After fiddling with it for a while, he began to work it carefully with his fingers, and modeled some little figures. The clay figures slowly began to change into flesh and bone, and then Esaugetuh Emissee breathed life into them. And that is how the first humans came to be."

A beautiful land

"But," pointed out the elder, "there was no place for these little creatures to live, for apart from the Master's own hill, the world was still covered with water. So Esaugetuh Emissee built an enormous mound. It was a bit like our sacred mound, only much, much bigger. It was so big that it covered the oceans.

"The Master of Breath carved out valleys and molded hills. He planted the woodlands and filled valleys and depressions with rivers and lakes. Then he set his newly modeled people on the beautiful land.

"Our Master's last task," explained the elder, "was to teach our people how to live at one with the land, how to fish from the creeks, and how to fight to protect our land, our families, and our traditions."

The elder described how the women learned which plants to use for food, how to plant corn, make medicines from roots and herbs, weave cloth, and mix colorful dyes.

"Esaugetuh's breath is in each of us," he said. "It is in the land and the plants that grow on it, and in all living things. Remember, always, that we give life to the land, and the land gives life to us. That is why you must always live in harmony with nature and all living creatures."

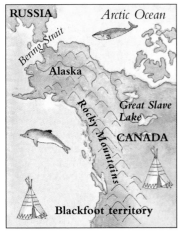

Old Man's Magic

The first North American peoples crossed from Asia to the northeastern tip of North America, where the Bering Strait is today, on bridges of land and ice. Native American myths are rarely about the creation of a universe from nothing. Instead, they deal with putting the finishing touches to a world that already existed, and with the origins of particular tribes.

The Blackfoot tribe packed up their buffalo tepees, their buckskin clothes, and their pots and pans. It was spring, and time to move on. The winter snows had melted from the northern plains. The buffalo herds, which the tribes hunted for meat and hides, had already migrated to the fresh, new growth of prairie grass.

Old Man, the Master of Life, had come from the south, too, when he was making the Blackfoot world. He roamed the plains and shaped the mountains and valleys. From the footprints he left behind him, water sprang and spread into lakes and flowing rivers. Where rivers and mountain met, shining cascades of water leapt sparkling in the morning light. Old Man brushed his hands over the new lands, covering the plains with waving grass where animals would graze. He daubed this rock red and another gold, and painted a rich landscape of woodland and prairie, marsh and scrub. When he had covered the plains with grass, and planted forests of pine, birch, and oak, Old Man set aside areas where wild roots, herbs, and berries would flourish. Now there was plenty of food for animals to eat.

Old Man led the bighorn sheep he had just made into the mountains. The bighorn sprang easily across rocks and deep gullies, his step sure and nimble.

As he traveled, Old Man made all kinds of animals and birds to live in his new land. He crafted lumps of clay into buffalo, which were to range in their thousands over the plains. He talked to the creatures and understood their language. Each bird and animal knew and loved Old Man.

Old Man's experiments

One of the new creatures was the bighorn sheep, with delicate legs and magnificent spiralling horns. Old Man proudly placed his latest creation on the ground, but the bighorn moved awkwardly, and didn't seem quite at home. So Old Man grasped a horn and led the bighorn high into the mountain pastures. As soon as he set it free, the animal sprang nimbly from rock to rock, and over deep gullies, and was fleet and sure of foot, even on the steepest of slopes. The bighorn lived in the mountains from that day.

Old Man's next experiment was the antelope, but this animal was not at all happy on the rough mountain ground. It slipped and slid and grazed its knees. So Old Man took the antelope back down the mountainside, and set it free to bound gracefully over the prairies.

The Blackfoot tribe came to the banks of the Milk River. "Let us rest awhile here," said the chief, "for this is the place where Old Man rested. He lay down on his back, face to the skies, arms stretched out. See the rocks over there? Those are the very stones that Old Man placed around his body to mark where he lay."

The tribe continued their journey towards the northern plains, past The Knees, a pair of rocky outcrops that rose from the Plains. "This is where Old Man tripped and fell," explained the chief. "He made rocks where his knees hit the ground."

Life from a handful of clay

The tribe came to a river at the foot of the Sweet Grass Hills. A child asked, "How did we come to be?"

The child's mother said, "Old Man picked up a handful of clay, like this from the river bank, and molded it into the shape of a woman and a child, just like you and me.

"Old Man left the lifeless figures on the ground and covered them up with some plants. Each day, he went to look at them, and each day they had changed a little to be even more like us. On the fourth day, Old Man told the figures to walk to the river with him.

"When they arrived at the river bank," the Blackfoot mother continued, "the first woman asked Old Man 'Will we live forever and ever?'. Old Man hadn't thought about this. He had just assumed that everything would live for ever, like he would.

"So the first woman told Old Man: 'Throw a stone into the river. If it floats, people will live forever, and if it sinks, then people will die and learn of suffering; they will pity each other.' "

The Blackfoot mother explained how Old Man made more men and women. He showed them how to gather roots and berries to eat. He taught them how to make weapons and tools, how to hunt animals and fish, and also how to make fire with sticks.

The Blackfoot boy asked: "How did we come to be?"

CONNECTIONS

• Old Man is a little like the ancestors of the Aborigines, who wandered over the land making water holes and plants, and naming birds and animals.

• Like the aboriginal people of Australia, too, the Native Americans migrated from another land to a world that already existed. There are also similarities between some Native American myths and those of central Asia, from where the first Americans came.

• In many living tribal myths, the journeys of the ancestors can be tracked in landscape features that still exist today.

Blackfoot tribe tepee camp in Alberta, western Canada, in 1890. The Blackfeet were a nomadic tribe who roamed the plains of North America in the shadow of the Rocky Mountains. They followed herds of buffaloes through the seasons. These large animals were eaten for their meat, and their hides were stretched and dried to make tepees. The Blackfeet were also renowned for their beautifully decorated buckskin clothing, which was made from softer deer hide.

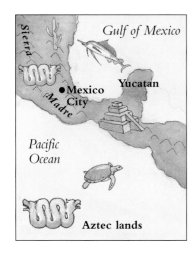

Five Aztec Worlds

The Aztecs believed that they lived in the fifth of a succession of earlier worlds that had been created and destroyed. They called their worlds "suns." Each sun was ruled by a particular god who was linked with a cosmic element—earth, wind, fire, and water. The gods and the elements they controlled created worlds, but they were also involved in destroying them.

The great Aztec creator god, Ometeotl, was both male and female. As the aeons of before-the-world-began rolled by, the god's jaw hung ever longer, and loose folds of skin hung from its bones. Far from being weakened by old age, Ometeotl's life force increased. He was able to produce the gods whose actions and conflicts would create the Aztec worlds.

The first gods were brothers who set about making the heavens, the Earth, the oceans, and the underworld. They fashioned the first human couple, introduced fire, and drew up a sacred calendar that logged days of sacrifice to be made to them.

Tezcatlipoca was appointed ruler of the first new world. He called his empire the "Sun of Earth," and peopled it with a race of giants so strong that they could pull up trees with their bare hands.

Tezcatlipoca was fiery by nature, the ruler of night, moon, and stars. Not for nothing did his name mean Black Smoking Mirror. Just as changing reflections are captured in a

Suddenly, a giant cat broke through the water's surface. It was Tezcatlipoca's new guise, the first of a deadly force of jaguars, sent to destroy the Earth.

mirror, so the god was forever changing his form. One of his brothers was the milder-natured Quetzalcoatl, a magnificent plumed serpent of iridescent emerald green. Quetzalcoatl was everything that Tezcatlipoca was not. He brought balance and harmony, life-giving water and sunlight, fertility and new life into the world. He was the god of wind and injected breath into all living things.

Sometimes the two brothers worked together as allies, at others they were locked in conflict.

Violent ends and new beginnings

After 676 heavenly years (each of which is over 250 times as long as one of our years) had passed, the time came for the first world of Tezcatlipoca to end. Quetzalcoatl raised a heavy staff and struck his brother, sending him hurtling into the sea. There was a silence. The wake from the god's fall stilled. Suddenly, a giant cat broke through the water's surface in an explosion of spray.

Now, a jaguar is the biggest wild cat found in South America today, but this one was a thousand times bigger. It was Tezcatlipoca's new guise. With him came a deadly force of snarling jaguars. Their job was to complete the destruction of the Sun of Earth. The powerful cats roamed the land and devoured the giants who lived there. When they had finished, Tezcatlipoca rose into the heavens and became the constellation known in the West as Ursa Major, or the Great Bear.

The creator god brothers started to make a new world. They called it the Sun of Wind, and the wind god, Quetzalcoatl, was the obvious choice for ruler. After 364 heavenly years, though, Tezcatlipoca returned to challenge his brother. He kicked him mercilessly and called up screaming winds that swept away the tropical forest world he had made and filled with humans. The few survivors turned into monkeys, and their descendants swing through the jungle today.

Tlaloc, the rain god, ruled over the next world, the Sun of Rain, for 312 heavenly years. Quetzalcoatl returned this time, and fought Tlaloc with his own

A couple hid in a hollow tree and escaped the flood that destroyed the fourth world.

weapon. It was a rain of lethal fire, like the red-hot ashes and lava bombs that spew out of volcanoes. The world and everything on it was demolished, apart from some humans who survived—and were changed into turkeys.

The fourth world was the Sun of Water, whose queen was the jade-skirted goddess of streams and lakes, Chalchiuhtlicue. A flood inundated the land and all that lived on it. The mountains dissolved and a leaden sky fell upon the Earth. People were transformed into fish. Only one man and woman escaped. They hid in a hollow tree that rose above the flood, nibbling heads of maize for food, and waited for the waters to recede.

End of the Aztec worlds

The fifth world was the one in which the Aztec people lived. It was the Sun of the Center, and it was ruled by Xiuhtecuhtli, the god of fire. The Aztecs believed their world would end in a devastating earthquake, for the odd number five is the number of instability. Instead, it all came to an end in 1521, when the last Aztec king, Montezuma, surrendered his empire to Spanish invaders led by Hernan Cortes. The Spanish—hungry for the legendary new world full of gold—conquered the people, and destroyed their civilization and culture.

CONNECTIONS

• The Aztecs won their empire by conquering the tribes who already lived there. In earlier times, though, they had been the underdogs, constantly driven from fertile land and forced to move on. Aztec myths tell a similar story of worlds that must be destroyed before new worlds can begin.

• A similar idea of worlds being created only to be destroyed, and new worlds created in their place, is echoed in Hindu mythology. Brahma taught that in an endless stream of time and space, universes are created and disappear.

• The Aztecs found fossilized remains of great beasts in their lands. These, they thought, were the bones of giants that remained after Tezcatlipoca's jaguars had eaten them.

The quetzal is a rare and beautiful bird that lives in the mountain jungles of Central America. It sheds and regrows its tail feathers after each breeding season. This cycle of growth and rebirth is similar to the Aztecs' view of creation. Quetzalcoatl took the form of a serpent clothed in the quetzal's brilliant plumage. In one myth, the god was killed by fire, and quetzal birds rose from the ashes.

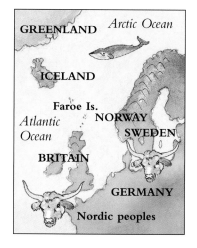

GREENLAND Arctic Ocean

ICELAND

Faroe Is.

Atlantic
Ocean NORWAY

SWEDEN

BRITAIN

GERMANY

Nordic peoples

Land of Ice

The Norse peoples migrated from central Asia to colonize Scandinavian lands long ago. The frozen landscape of the creation myth recalls the ice-bound world they encountered. The conflicts of the gods echo the battles that must have taken place between rival tribes. This tale is recorded in a collection of Norse mythological stories called the Edda.

The land of ice was wreathed in a swirling mist in the moisture-laden gloom. There was neither sky nor sea, not a grain of soil, nor a single blade of grass. The frozen grey plain was split by a jagged slash like an open wound. Here, where it was too steep for ice to form, bare rocks, silvered with freezing droplets of moisture, dropped into the immense abyss of Ginnungagap, and cliffs plunged into a dizzying void. The chasm wound its way from Niflheim, the land of ice, far to the south until it reached the land of fire, Muspelsheim.

Birth from ice

Rivers flowed freely from the warm south, but when they came to the land of ice, they froze solid. Layers of frozen river piled up into immense glaciers, filling Ginnungagap to its broken rims. Then came the first spring. Warm winds blew in from the fiery south, and breathed over the ice so that melted water glazed the surface. It was the beginning of life on Earth.

Audhumla the cow provided milk for Ymir, the frost giant, which gave him strength.

In one place, droplets of water containing the elements of life began to merge and take on the form of a giant figure. It was Ymir, the frost giant, who had the power to create all living creatures and plants. In another place, more water droplets gathered, and the giant cow they call Audhumla rose from them.

Audhumla was the first-ever animal and provider of food. Milk streamed from her udders, and Ymir drank his fill and grew strong. As for the cow, she grazed the ice, and the salt within it gave her sustenance. Melted water trickled from her warm tongue and gathered into a pool. Hair sprouted here, and then a huge head appeared. Soon, the mighty frame of another giant reared from the ice sheet.

The newcomer was called Buri, who—like Ymir—was able to create life. His son Bor married the giantess Bestla, a daughter of Ymir. From these two came the first great gods of the northern lands: Odin, Vili, and Ve.

Ymir was still reproducing busily. From the sweat that fell from his body sprang a line of cruel frost giants. They had human bodies but terrifying, superhuman strength.

Giants and gods battle for blood

The frost giants and the great gods were at loggerheads right from the start. The giants kept trying to win supreme power for themselves, but Odin, Vili, Ve, and

CONNECTIONS

• Other myths in which the body of a vanquished god is changed into parts of the Earth include Pan Gu of China, and Tiamat, the Mesopotamian sea goddess.

• Yggdrasil was an ash tree. The ash was also the sacred tree of Poseidon, the Greek god of the sea. Another name for Odin—who also became god of seafarers—is Yggra, from which Yggdrasil comes. The word is similar to *hygra*, the ancient Greek word for water.

Cows graze in the high mountain pastures of Scandinavia, near a glacier. Like the first cow, Audhumla, who provided food for her master, cows have been a vital source of food throughout Scandinavian history.

their descendants
always bounced back.
Nevertheless, the gods
wanted to make a good and
stable world. The only way,
they all agreed, was to get
rid of the original creator
of them all, Ymir. They
hauled the giant to the chasm
of Ginnungagap and
slaughtered him mercilessly.
Blood gushed into the abyss.
Ginnungagap was flowing
once again, only this time
with a torrent of blood
so fierce that all but
two of the frost giants
were drowned in it.
The survivors made
themselves a canoe
and paddled away to
safety on the bloody
river. They would
father a new race of
giants, which would
return one day to
plague the gods.

Recycled god
The last of Ymir's
blood flowed from
his body and
gathered in a ring
around the world to
form the oceans. His flesh
became soil, and his bones
turned to mountains and
rock. The great gods built
the roof of the heavens
with the giant's
skull. Ymir's brain
dissolved into
clouds that would

*Yggdrasil is the universal tree
of Norse myth, in whose shade
the whole of Earth lies.*

race across the skies forever.
Until this time, sparks from the
hot lands of the south had scattered
randomly in all directions. Now, they
were contained by the roof of the sky
and became the sun, moon, and stars.
The conquering gods organized the
seasons, and for day to follow night. Finally,
from logs on the seashore, they carved man
and woman, and called them Ask and Embla.
Odin breathed life into the humans. Vili gave
them emotions and intelligence, while Ve
granted them speech, hearing, and sight.
The Universe that the gods made was like a
giant ash tree, which they called Yggdrasil. The
whole of Earth lies in Yggdrasil's shade, and
the topmost branches stretch into the
heavens. The tree's roots plunge into the
depths of the Earth to the kingdom of
the goddess Hel and to Niflheim, the
icy lands of the dead. Enchanted
dew falls on Yggdrasil, keeping it
evergreen and eternally alive.

Order from Chaos

Creation stories gave the ancient Greeks a sense of the past and explained their world. They also provided a stage set for the coming of humans. Each aspect of the physical world—the Earth, the Heavens, thunder, and lightning—had its god, and soon there were more gods who represented emotions, feelings, and the worst fears humans could ever imagine. All are described as if they were people.

Before the Universe came into being, there was nothing that you could actually describe, only chaos. There were no living plants or creatures, no land, no people—only felt-black darkness, space, and swirling matter. Slowly, shapes began to form and the Universe began to organize itself into different parts, like the pieces of a puzzle slotting into place. Gaia, the Earth, and mother of all things, emerged from the confusion, but beneath her crusty surface, the god Chaos still reigned in a world of molten rock.

Gaia lay still and asleep for a long while, but feelings of love and desire were moving in her. They arose from her, and Eros, the god of desire, was born. Eros stirred things up so that different forces were attracted to each other and new life could be created. Gaia's own desire swelled and brought forth the god of the Heavens, Ouranos. Gaia placed him in the empty space that lay above her, to be master of the skies. Ouranos loved Gaia and showered her with rain, so that she became sweet and rich, and carpeted with trees and flowers.

Mountains reared from the Earth's surface, as Gaia heaved again and again in the labor of creation. Beneath her, Chaos was busy producing other gods and spirits, so that bit by bit, the elements of the world came into being. Nyx was his first daughter. She had twin children—Hemera and Aether.

Nyx, the goddess of night, gave birth to twins who were filled with light.

Hemera, goddess of the day, took turns with her mother Nyx in joining with the sky, so that the eternal cycle of light and darkness on Earth was set up. Her twin brother, Aether, brought pure, clear, ethereal light to the heavenly atmosphere high above the land.

Heaven and Earth—Ouranos and Gaia—seemed inseparable. They had one child after another. Among them were twelve Titans, brothers and sisters of gargantuan proportions, who were the first creatures to live on Earth. The Titans' main job was to produce the gods and spirits who would interfere with human life when it came. Kronos was the last-born, and it was to him that Gaia eventually turned for help.

"I'm completely worn out by your father Ouranos's constant attentions and all this childbirth," she complained. She handed him a sickle. Its curved blade glinted cruelly.

"Strike Ouranos with this so that I can have some peace," she ordered.

Murder most foul

Kronos was more than willing. He knew that by killing his father, he would gain power for himself. When the unsuspecting Ouranos next approached Gaia, Kronos struck. The blood that gushed from the dying god was filled with magical powers. Wherever it splattered upon the land, giants and spirits exploded into being. Three avenging Furies were born in this way. They were to avenge the crime that Kronos had committed against his father. For the rest of time, from their home in the Underworld, they delivered dreadful punishments upon those who committed crimes. Some good also came from Ouranos's blood. Where a crimson drop fell into a swelling wave in the sea, a beautiful woman arose from the foam. She was Aphrodite, the goddess of love.

Kronos raised the sickle and brought it crashing down onto his father's head.

A dreadful curse

For a time, Kronos had what he wanted. His father was dead and he had supreme command of the Universe. He married his sister, Rhea, and wanted to start a family. But Ouranos had laid a terrible curse on him in his dying breath:

"The time will come when this will happen to you too," the old god had gasped. "Just as you destroyed me, so you will be slaughtered by one of your very own children."

Kronos feared his own death even more than he wanted children. The only solution he could think of was to get rid of each child as soon as it was born— before it had a chance to threaten him.

Rhea delivered one baby after another—Hestia, Demeter, Hera, Hades, Poseidon. Each time, Kronos snatched the newborn and devoured it in one gulp, swaddling clothes and all. Rhea was devastated. How could she save her children from this ghastly fate? She swore that her next baby would survive. When it was due, she fled to a faraway island. There, in the darkest hour of the night, she delivered her third son. His name was Zeus.

Unfortunately, Kronos knew that the baby was due, so Rhea had to act quickly. She fled to the island of Crete and went high into the mountains. ▶

All the gods were so busy reproducing that there were soon enough gods and spirits to cover every aspect of life on Earth. Helios and Selene governed the sun and moon. Dark Thanatos was master of death, while the gentle Hypnos commanded sleep. Exquisite nymphs brought the rosy dawn and evening sunset, and fierce spirits stirred up storms and raging seas. A host of evil demons introduced such miseries as deceit, old age, forgetfulness, and famine to the world. Soon there was a representative for every experience, feeling, emotion, and terror you can imagine.

CONNECTIONS

• In many myths, a violent separation enables the process of creation to move onto the next stage. The slaying of Ouranos paved the way for Kronos to be master of the Universe, and for the Olympian gods to take center stage. In the Maori creation story, it is only when the gods of Earth and sky are wrenched apart that life can begin.

• Many cultures tell of gods turning into star constellations. The Aztec god Tezcatlipoca became the group of stars that is known in the West as Ursa Major (the Great Bear).

• The idea of night coming into existence first, before day, is typical of many European myths, including Nordic legends told in Scandinavia and Germany.

Order from Chaos

There she laid Zeus in a cradle of gold and hid him in a cave. She asked her mother, Gaia, to protect her little boy while she went to face Kronos. Somehow, she had to trick her husband into believing that she was bringing him their newborn child. She found a smooth rock about the same weight as a baby, and wrapped it in swaddling clothes so that it looked just like all the previous babies, and presented the bundle of clothes to Kronos. Wasting no time, Kronos took the bundle, threw back his head, opened his throat and swallowed the whole lot.

"That's the end of that little problem," he thought.

Rhea was still worried. Kronos was, after all, ruler of Earth and sky, and might spot the living child and guess the truth. The golden cradle was therefore hung from a tree, so that it was neither on Earth, nor in the sky, nor in the sea, but in a kind of nowhere place.

Now babies are not, by their nature, silent. They gurgle, laugh and cry. Zeus was no exception. So just outside the cave, Rhea stationed a couple of warriors, not to guard Zeus, but to cover up any noise he made. The warriors made a barrier of sound with their crashing shields and swords as they practiced fighting.

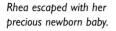

Rhea escaped with her precious newborn baby.

Two beautiful and gentle nymphs looked after the baby and fed him on milk and honey. As he grew up, the danger of discovery passed, and Zeus would wander among the thyme-scented and sun-filled hills with the local shepherds.

Revenge of the children

When he was a man, though, Zeus knew that he was destined to do a very important job. He went to his mother, Rhea. "I have a plan to bring back all my brothers and sisters who were swallowed," he said. "Can you get me a job as father's cup-bearer? Kronos won't know me as his son—he doesn't even know of my existence."

Rhea did as he suggested. Zeus took his father's drinks to him every day, and Kronos soon learned to trust his new employee. The time had come to put the next part of the plan into action. Rhea mixed a very special drink and handed it to her son. It was sweet-tasting, like honey, but it contained an ingredient that would make Kronos sick.

As he did every day, Zeus handed the drink to his unsuspecting father. Kronos liked the flavor and knocked it back in one gulp. Suddenly, his body doubled up and he was violently sick. He vomited out the baby-weight rock and every one of his children he had devoured.

The gods of Mount Olympus

The children escaped and soon took the form of fully fledged gods. They met up with Zeus and plotted to do away with Kronos for good.

Hades put on his helmet of darkness and became invisible. He crept into Kronos's palace and stole the king's weapons. Now it was safe for Poseidon and Zeus.

CONNECTIONS
• The Olympian gods were humans on a grand scale—they had human emotions, failings, and weaknesses, but with supernatural powers. Their inventions—from fire and metalworking, to music and wine-making—built the human world.
• For the ancient Greeks, the world is revolves around and is made for humans. This is different from some tribal communities, whose myths reflect their belief that humans, animals, and even plants are all of equal importance.

The twin summits of Mount Olympus in Northern Greece are accessible only to serious hikers today. They are called the Pantheon and the Throne of Zeus, and they are often hidden by layers of cloud. Olympus is Greece's highest mountain.

Poseidon brandished his three-forked trident, and Kronos reeled back. Zeus then struck his father with the full force of his own devastating weapon—a bolt of lightning.

The prophecy of Ouranos had come true: Zeus had destroyed his father and was now king god. He and his brothers divided up the Universe. Poseidon ruled the sea, and Hades was given the Underworld. Zeus himself was supreme lord of the sky and the father of all

The infant Zeus was laid in a golden cradle that hung in a tree. Beautiful nymphs fed him with milk and honey, and a pair of warriors fought mock battles to mask the sound of his cries.

humankind. The dominion of the Earth was shared by the twelve gods and goddesses who lived on the Greek mountain Olympus. They were called the Olympians, and they would soon be involved in a host of extraordinary adventures and meddlings in earthly life.

The world was ready for the coming of humans.

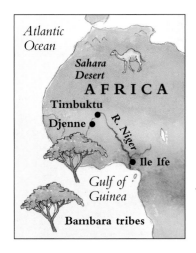

The Evil Thorn Tree

The Bambara people live in the upper reaches of the River Niger in West Africa. Their myths explain how their world and people came to be, but are also a framework for day-to-day living. Creation is not a single, isolated event, but an ongoing process. Things are constantly being spun into existence.

Before time and knowledge, there was only silence. No darkness or light, nothing that was solid, no water or movement. There were not even spirits—only a still silence.

At the very heart of the silence, something stirred, like the smallest gasp of breath or a rustle deep in the forest undergrowth: "Yo."

It was the Cosmic Word, the sound at the very root of creation. Yo came from nothing and swelled into a sigh, and then into a whirlwind of sound that reverberated throughout the silent cosmos.

This was the force that set creation into action. Wisdom, knowledge, and understanding were gathered together into Yo, so that new life could exist—and the world was ready to begin in earnest.

The greedy wood spirit

First of all, Earth and sky were spun from the whirl of energy, but there were still no recognizable shapes or beings, order of seasons, and day and night. Not until Yo sent an acacia seed (some say it was just a lump of wood) and a body of water spiraling down to Earth.

This is how Pemba, the wood spirit, and Faro, who ruled the waters, came to be. Pemba found some soil and shaped it into the first woman, Musso-Koroni, They had many, many children who were the first animals and people.

Pemba wanted to become the supreme god, in absolute control of the waters, the Earth, and the Universe. He needed blood, in huge quantities, to build his strength.

"Musso-Koroni," Pemba commanded in a thunderous voice, "come with me now to the Earth-swamp, and plant me in the soil beneath the murky waters."

His wife obeyed, and Pemba grew into a mighty thorn tree. Pemba was the first tree and king of all trees, but he was also very selfish and greedy for power.

"Musso-Koroni," he bellowed, "I want a constant supply of blood. Slaughter our children and sacrifice them to me in recognition of my supremacy."

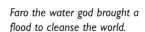

Faro the water god brought a flood to cleanse the world.

CONNECTIONS

• Look for other stories in which a word or breath triggers creation into action. In many mythologies, there is a powerful sacred word. The Hindu faith has the word "Om," and "Chi" is the original breath that kick-started the Chinese Universe.

• Pemba's insatiable greed for power and bloodthirsty actions spoiled the first attempt at creation—it was imperfect and had to be made pure again by a great flood. There are cleansing floods in Mesopotamian and Judeo-Christian traditions, too. In the Bible, after the first people had discovered evil, the good man, Noah, and a pair of each creature on Earth survived the flood by living on a big boat called an ark.

The acacia is just one of many thorny plants that grow in the African bush country. The thorns try to protect the trees from being eaten by grazing animals. Some acacia trees have particularly lethal thorns when they are young. This might have inspired the story of Pemba as an evil thorn tree.

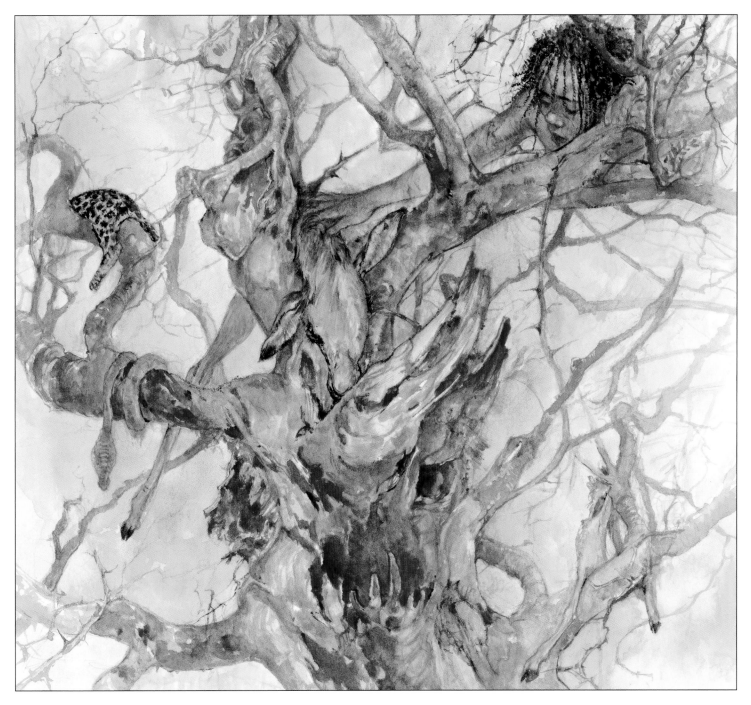

Blood power

Pemba knew that with every drop of blood that was spilled in his name, he would become stronger and stronger, giving him more and more power.

His wife obediently brought him a chain of slaughtered animals and humans. She even shed blood herself, for whenever she came close, she tore herself on the evil thorns that lurked among the tangled branches. Finally, she could stand it no more, and left her husband for good. For the rest of time, Musso-Koroni wandered through the world, leaving a trail of disorder and misery in her wake.

Faro now had to challenge Pemba's bid for power. He could no longer stand by and watch all this slaughter and evil going on. As the water spirit, part of his job was to keep things alive, but he also knew that he could wreak

Musso-Koroni fed the evil wood spirit Pemba a bloody diet of slaughtered animals and humans to increase his power.

disaster. So Faro gathered his waters into a deep and devastating flood that worked down into the evil thorn tree's roots and loosened them. Pemba was uprooted and completely destroyed.

Healing waters

The flood cleansed the world of evil, and Faro was able to make a fresh start. He brought order, gave names to the creatures and plants that he made, and taught people how to farm so that they would not starve.

Balance came to the world, and ever since, the rhythm of daily life has been thanks to the efforts of Faro and his spirits. They return to Earth every 400 years, to tidy it up and restore harmony.

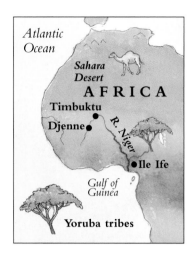

Atlantic Ocean

Sahara Desert

A F R I C A

Timbuktu

Djenne

R. Niger

Ile Ife

Gulf of Guinea

Yoruba tribes

Obtalala and the Hen

The Yoruba people are one of the biggest ethnic groups in West Africa. There are many different clans, each with their own versions of traditional stories. Myths and rituals are adapted to fit in with each clan's lifestyle and history, as well as the lives of the people and their clan ancestors.

Orisa-nla came first, before the gods and spirits. The essence of everything was contained in Orisa-nla.

Atunda was Orisa-nla's servant. It seemed as if he always had to do as he was told, and that the only reason for his existence was to be a slave. But he had a very important part to play in making the Universe. After all, his name did mean "something that destroys and creates again…."

One time, in the unformed Universe, Atunda saw Orisa-nla at the foot of a cosmic hill.

"This is my chance to rebel," thought Atunda.

He found the biggest meteorite in the Universe, and then he sent it careering down the hillside. It crashed into Orisa-nla, causing him to explode into myriad pieces. As the fragments of Orisa-nla hurtled into Space, each one was miraculously reborn as a spirit. And each spirit—or orisha, as the Yoruba people say—held the secret of divine wisdom.

Even spirits get bored

The orishas lived in the Heavens at first. All that lay beneath them was a gleaming sheet of motionless water, bathed in eternal twilight. The water world was enshrouded by mists, and stretched to infinity in every direction. There were no people there, no plants, no animals—because there was no dry land.

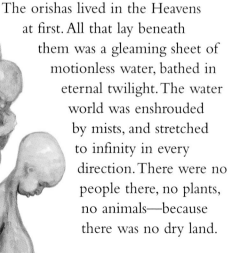

Some of the little clay models that Obtalala made were perfect, but other models were deformed.

The head orisha was Olodumare, owner of the sky. He was invisible but everywhere, all-seeing and all-knowing. Each of the other spirits had particular powers. Obtalala's speciality was the power to create new life. The problem was, he had nowhere to put it. Obtalala decided to confront all-knowing Olodumare.

"We need to make dry land, so that living things can be made," he announced. "Besides, the orishas are bored and need something to do."

It was Orunmilla, however, the spirit of wisdom, who produced a workable plan.

"Fill a snail shell with sand," he told Obtalala. "Conjure up a white hen, a palm nut, and a black cat, and take these to the water world."

Now some say that a thousand silken cobwebs arched over the marsh world, on which the orishas could abseil down from the skies. For his mission, though, Obtalala commissioned the goldsmith spirit to make him a chain of gold. When the chain was finished, he slung a bag containing the hen, palm nut, and cat over his shoulder, and began to climb down the chain. He left the crystal light of the Heavens and passed into the twilight marsh world.

The hen and the palm nut

Eventually, he heard the waters beneath him, and immediately emptied the sand from the giant shell. A vast mound rose above the waters. Now, Obtalala put the white hen to work. When he placed the bird on the mound, she immediately began scratching and kicking the sand, sending it flying in all directions. In some places, just a few grains landed, or scattered evenly over wide areas; in others it piled high. So it was that hills and valleys, plains and mountains were formed. Where no sand fell, there were flowing rivers, or the giant pools of lakes and seas.

The hen finished building the Earth in four days. On the fifth day, Obtalala stepped onto the newly formed land and called the place Ife. Obtalala built the first house on Ife and called it Ile.

Olodumare, the Master of the sky, was impressed with Obtalala's new world. As a reward, he let the sun cross the sky every day. Each day saw the coming of warmth and light, day and night, rainfall and the seasons, and things could grow. Obtalala planted the palm nut, and the world's first trees grew and bore fruit. There were palm nuts to make oil, and palm juice to drink.

It wasn't enough, though. Obtalala was bored and lonely without company. One day, he decided to mold little figures of men and women from the clay soil. He used the shape of his own body for inspiration, and after he had made several, he took a drink of palm wine. And then another. And another. He didn't stop modeling, even when he was completely out of control. Eventually, Obtalala fell into a drunken sleep. When he woke up, he gazed in horror at the figures. Some were misshapen or had limbs missing. This is how it came to be that some people are born with deformities. Obtalala was so appalled at what he had done, that he swore he would protect people who were crippled, deaf, blind, or malformed in any way, forever.

The white hen of cosmic proportions scratched in the sand., and the grains settled to form hills, mountains, and plains.

Meanwhile, his pile of clay figures, perfect and imperfect ones, were still lifeless. Only the head orisha, Olodumare, who was the owner of the sky had the power to breathe life into things. Obtalala thought this was unfair since he had done all the work. He decided to spy on Olodumare to see how he gave life. But the all-knowing god put Obtalala into a deep sleep. He didn't wake him up until all the little figures had come to life as real people. The humans lived to be very old, weak, and racked with pain. They prayed to Olodumare to release them, and this is why he introduced death. Other orishas came to live in Obtalala's world. These spirits live still, deep within each person, and in every place and every living thing.

CONNECTIONS

• As in many world religions, the Yoruba believe that there is one all-seeing, all-knowing god, Olodumare, and that nothing can be hidden from a god who sees the inside and outside of humans.

• Through ritual dances and acts, the Yoruba people keep sacred spirits alive and part of daily life. They see every aspect of their lives as a continual process of being crushed and reborn. Their rituals are also a way of renewing themselves. Through them, they can return to being whole and starting anew, just as the orishas in the story are born from the shattered Orisa-nla.

The Yoruba people live mainly in the coastal regions of West Africa and in Nigeria near the River Niger. The town of Ile Ife is their most sacred town.

Birth from Water

Ancient Egypt was a country of rival city-states. Every city-state had its own god and its own myths, recounting how their particular world and gods came to be. This story comes from the town of Heliopolis (whose name means "city of the sun"), in a place that is now a suburb of the modern city of Cairo.

From Atum's breath were born Shu, god of air, and Tefnut, goddess of rain— the essences of life.

Nun was an infinite ocean. It was there instead of the Earth, the sky, and the stars. The waters were dark, empty, and motionless, until, in a surge of parting waves, a mound of solid land—something like the islands you can see on the River Nile today—arose from the waters. Next, a giant lotus flower pushed its way through the soil. And, as its crown of waxy petals opened, the creator god Atum emerged from its center.

The breath of life

Atum needed help. It was a big responsibility, being the first, the absolute beginning of everything. He needed to make more gods who could help him start piecing together the world. So he summoned his strength, and breathed out in a steamy whoosh. It was like a puff of breath on a frosty morning—only on a universal scale! In the billowing cloud of breath, two ghostly forms emerged. The air became Shu, god of air. Myriad droplets of moisture joined and formed into Tefnut, goddess of rain.

There wasn't a lot of universe-building that Tefnut and Shu could do on their own, without essential ingredients such as the sun, plants, and animals. So they spent their time exploring the protective waters of the ocean, Nun. But Nun was vast and dark—and the young gods were soon completely lost in her fathomless depths.

Atum was frantic. His eyes were like rolling fiery disks, as they penetrated every corner of the primeval seas. Eventually, Shu and Tefnut were found in a distant, gloomy abyss. Atum wept with relief to see his children again. As his divine tears slowly fell through the void, each one miraculously turned into a human being.

The parting of Earth and sky

The beginnings of Earth existed, but were yet to be fully formed. It was time for Shu and Tefnut to have children who could add something more to creation. They had twins—the Earth god, Geb, and the sky goddess, Nut. The two were inseparable. Nut arched over her beloved Earth, with her feet on one horizon and her hands on the other. Shu was jealous of the twins' love for each other, and became so irritated that he tore them apart.

"You live separately from now on," he ordered. "You can get together once a day, and no more."

From that time onward, every night, the sky goddess Nut gently falls to Earth and enfolds her twin in an embrace. That is when darkness comes. Sometimes, Nut is so desperate to be with her twin, that she goes to him in daytime. When this happens, storm clouds gather and the sky darkens as night casts a shadow over the sunlight.

Rivals for power

Atum, the creator god, continued making things, such as plants and insects, reptiles and other creatures that live on the ground, but his power was declining as younger gods

The sky goddess Nut arched over her beloved Geb, who was the Earth.

took control of the Universe. The sun god Ra was at his peak strength in those early days of the world. Some say that he was born from Atum himself, others say that he rose from the gods Nut and Geb, Earth and sky.

Ra rose every morning, from a beautiful, blue-petalled lotus bud that pierced the surface of the ocean Nun. He was joined by Shu, god of air, and the pair of them traveled through the land of Egypt, bringing light and life to each of the provinces in turn. Their journey took 12 hours—the 12 hours of daylight. Then Ra returned to the lotus flower and was enclosed within its petals as they, and night, folded.

In his turn, Ra, too, became old and retired to the Heavens when he was replaced by younger, stronger gods. He still makes his daily journey though, rising above the eastern horizon, and sailing across the ocean of the skies in his boat, the *Barque of a Million Years*. At sunset, he sails over the western horizon into the Underneath Sky.

CONNECTIONS

• Water is seen as the first element of creation in several mythologies. Before the world of the Yoruba people of West Africa came into being, there was a watery waste, and the first gods of Mesopotamian myth were the fresh and salt waters.

• The Egyptian way of life has always focussed on the River Nile for fertile river soils and water supply, and for communication and transportation. In bringing rainfall and water to the world, the god Tefnut also brought order—an order and a way of life that was dictated by the annual flooding of this great river.

• In later myths, Ra was depicted as the falcon-god, Horus. The Egyptians believed that animals had special powers and that the creator gods lived within them.

The lotus flower is a symbol of fertility, because it comes into bloom as the river rises in its annual flooding.

Marduk and the Tablets of Destiny

This story is taken from the Enuma Elish—an epic poem that describes the creation of the world and the foundation of its great capital city, Babylon. The earliest versions of the myth date from about 2000 BC.

Enuma elish la nabu shaman, which means "before the heavens above were named," describes a time when there were no reed beds or reed huts like the ones found by the mighty rivers Tigris and Euphrates. There was no land at all, there were not even any gods, just an endless sea enshrouded by a primeval mist.

But there was movement in the waters. Fresh water, called Apsu, and salt water, Tiamat, met and merged in a surge of effervescence and became one. New life sprang from the agitated waters, and from the foam came several very boisterous young gods. These children of the seas played and fought, laughed and shouted, as they surged back and forth in the primeval waters. They gave their parents no rest at all. Finally, their freshwater father had had his sleep disturbed once too often.

"I've had enough," Apsu announced to his saltwater wife. "I'm going to get rid of them."

"You can't do that," cried Tiamat. "They're our children. Let them be, they're only having fun!"

Her words had no effect whatsoever on Apsu, who was determined to silence his children for good. One of the young gods, called Ea, was suspicious. He had been born with the power of knowing everything, and he saw into Apsu's mind. Now Ea was destined to be the god of wisdom, cunning, and spells. He knew that if he could destroy Apsu first, he could seize the crown and mantle of radiant light—the symbols of power. Then he would rule the waters, too.

Ea gazed into the depths of his father's fresh waters and cast a spell that stilled Apsu into a deep sleep. Then he destroyed Apsu's soul, and grabbed the glistening crown and mantle. He and his wife Damkina promptly moved into Apsu's freshwater kingdom, settled down and had a son named Marduk.

An incredible son

It was clear from the start that there was something special about Marduk, and his proud parents brought in all the best-qualified goddesses to help raise their son. When he was fully grown, Marduk was bigger and more perfectly formed than any other god that had ever existed. Amazing strength flowed through every part of his body, and when he spoke, fire gushed from his mouth. In addition, Marduk had two pairs of blazing eyes that could see through everything, and two pairs of enormous, all-hearing ears. ▶

In the beginning, there was no land at all, just an endless sea enshrouded by a primeval mist. But new life sprang from the mixing of salt and fresh waters.

Marduk the magnificent filled his body with fire and mounted the Chariot of Storms, drawn by Flyer, Racer, Pitiless, and Slayer.

Marduk and the Tablets of Destiny

Trouble was stirring. The gods were splitting into factions. There were those who supported the old order of primordial chaos, and there was Ea and the forward-looking, fair gods of the celestial court of Anu, the sky deity. The fair gods were relieved that Ea had destroyed their intolerant father. But the gods who had not wanted change were angry and jealous of Ea's power. What was most irritating of all was that Ea's son, Marduk, was such a splendid and strapping young god that he completely outshone everyone else.

Marduk claimed the Tablets of Destiny as his spoils of war.

Revenge is planned

The disgruntled gods put their heads together and decided to stir their mother Tiamat into such a fury that she would avenge their father's death.

Tiamat, the ocean and first mother of the gods, was the only one who could possibly mount such a challenge. The rebels sought out their mother and set their plan in motion.

"Ea killed your husband Apsu," they taunted. "You should take your revenge by getting rid of that stuck-up son of his, Marduk."

It didn't take much to arouse Tiamat's anger. Soon she was preparing for all-out war, gathering all the forces of chaos to help her. She built an army of dreadful demons and monsters—the giant Rabid Dog, with its staring eyes and foaming mouth, the black-armored Scorpion Man with his deadly, stinging curve of tail, and the vicious Horned Viper Dragon.

Conditions of combat

Tiamat had another card up her sleeve. She still held the Tablets of Destiny, which gave her supreme power over the Universe. She decided to hand these to her new lover, Kingu, so that she could focus all her might on the battle ahead.

The fair gods didn't stand a chance against such a dreadful force. Their only hope lay in Marduk. But what was in it for him?

"I will challenge Tiamat on one condition," announced Marduk, "that when I have destroyed her, I shall hold the Tablets of Destiny and be Master of the Universe forever after, and that my word shall be obeyed without question."

The fair gods were so relieved that someone was going to sort things out for them, that they happily agreed to Marduk's demands.

Marduk prepared for battle. He filled his whole body with fire, slung a giant bow and arrow across his back, and carried a massive mace, a bolt of lightning, and a vast net. He called upon the winds of the Universe, and mounted the Chariot of Storms, drawn by the four beasts Flyer, Racer, Pitiless, and Slayer.

Battling against the elements

Nevertheless, when he was faced with the raging specter of Tiamat and her monstrous force, Marduk hesitated, suddenly afraid. How could he destroy such power?

CONNECTIONS

• The mixing of waters to stir creation into being is similar to the man and woman of Japanese myth stirring waters with their spears. In the Babylonian myths, it is the opposites—of salt and fresh waters—that trigger change; in Japan, the opposites of calm and rough waters are the catalyst.

• Ea's taming of the waters reflects the real world of the first civilizations in the valleys of the Tigris and Euphrates. Periods of flooding were followed by drought, and rivers were controlled by irrigation so that civilization could become established.

The text of the Enuma Elish, which gives this story of the creation of the world, was found in an ancient library built by the Babylonian king, Ashurbanipal, in the city of Niniveh. It was inscribed on clay tablets in a form of writing called cuneiform.

Tiamat sneered at him in contempt, which had the immediate effect of enraging Marduk. His courage restored, he challenged Tiamat to single combat. First, he cast his mighty net to surround the awesome ocean goddess. Then the winds attacked her with a mighty storm. Tiamat opened her mouth and she consumed the storm in one gulp. But it stuck and swelled in her belly, stretching it to the bursting point. Tiamat gasped in agony. As her mouth opened again, Marduk shot an arrow down her throat and killed her.

Earth rises from death

Tiamat's monsters were powerless without her, and Marduk immediately forced Kingu to hand over the Tablets of Destiny. The conquering god then turned back to Tiamut's body. With a single blow from his heavy mace, he shattered her skull and cut through the arteries that carried her blood. He sliced the body in two, and it separated like the two halves of a clam shell. With one half he made the canopy of sky, the other he lay over the deepwater kingdom of Apsu to form solid land. Tiamat's spittle turned into clouds and rain, and her eyes became the great rivers of Mesopotamia—the Tigris and the Euphrates.

From Tiamat's slain body, the elements of the Earth were formed. The most important rivers of Mesopotamia – the Tigris and the Euphrates – flowed from her eyes. Mesopotamia was known among early civilizations as the Land of the Two Rivers.

The new order

Marduk was now supreme lord of the Universe and king of the gods. He immediately began to put the Universe in order. He allotted a part of the Heavens to each of the fair gods—which are the constellations of stars in the sky you can see today. Then he made up a calendar of seasons, days, and months for the Earth, so that plants could flourish in a cycle of growth and regrowth.

Marduk was quite exhausted when he had finished. An idea came to him that would give the gods a break from their never-ending tasks of creation.

"I shall build a creature of blood and bone, and call him Human," he declared. "The human race can serve the gods by doing all the work on Earth. In that way, we gods can take a very well-deserved break from all of our hard toil."

This is how the human race began. The descendants of that first man lived from generation to generation, until this very day.

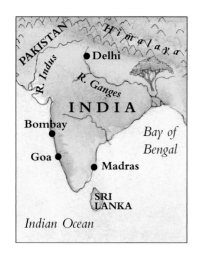

Gods and Lotus Flowers

From ancient times, India's holy men adapted traditional stories to explain their spiritual experiences in terms that ordinary people could understand. In India's main religion, Hinduism, thousands of different stories evolved, starring a host of gods and demons, wise people and heroes. All, though, have the common belief that there is a continuing cycle of creation and destruction, of life and death.

A new universe is waiting to unfold. Everything is motionless. The god Vishnu, blue-skinned and perfectly formed, lies asleep, graceful and absolutely still, on a bed formed by the thick coils of a giant cobra. Vishnu is always there, from the beginning, to kickstart every universe, for it is he who provides the creative energy that makes things happen. Ananta, the cobra, is the cosmic substance, carrying the elements of all living things. The serpent's body is without end, and its thousand hooded heads rear above Vishnu to shelter him.

Ananta is floating on an ocean of milk. No ripple of movement disturbs the ocean, either on its surface or in its unknown depths. The opaque waters stretch to infinity—flat, featureless, and silent.

Harmonious pair

A new dawn flushed the Universe and the waters pink. Vishnu was still lying on his back, when a green shoot pushed up through his navel. It grew into a long stem topped by a lotus bud, and Lakshmi, the goddess of the lotus flower emerged. Now there were two, male and female: Vishnu, who is in everything, the preserver of all the universes to come, and Lakshmi, who carries fertility and harmony, prosperity and good fortune. She is the perfect partner for Vishnu.

Vishnu lay on a bed formed by the coils of Ananta the cobra, while a wonderful lotus bud emerged from his navel.

Manual for living

Before the Universe begins, there must be rules to guide how it should be formed and how life should be lived. This was to be Brahma's job.

The bud unfolded into a wide, shallow bowl, which was ringed by a thousand golden petals. Sitting at their center, cross-legged, was Brahma, his body glowing with the creative force within it. Four arms radiated from his body, and in each of his four hands was a book. Fortunately, Brahma also had four heads—one to read each book. The books contained the sacred laws of the Veda, which would guide humans on how they should live on Earth.

Who am I?

So Brahma the creator had his manuals on how to build and run the Universe. When the lesser gods came into being, they would always go to Brahma for guidance. But there was still a nagging question in his mind.

"Who am I?" he wondered aloud.

No one answered, for no one else was there. All that Brahma could see was the beautiful lotus flower, which was surrounded by water.

"I wonder if this lotus is actually attached to anything." Brahma decided that he would investigate further. He lowered himself inside the light-green funnel of stem. But when he reached the bottom of the stem, he could see no Vishnu, no serpent, he could see absolutely nothing.

All Brahma could do was to go back to his lotus seat and think deeply. He closed his eyes and focussed his mind and went into a state of meditation. He searched inside himself for the meaning of why he was there. The god Vishnu appeared to him in his trancelike state, and spoke.

"What you need to do," Vishnu explained, "is to live a very strict life, and to eat and drink only what you need to for survival. That will create a fire and energy within you, which will help you to create."

When he came out of his deep meditation, Brahma knew what to do, even though there was still nothing in the world. All the vital ingredients were around him, like atoms, left over from the Universe that had gone before. They just had to be recreated—and Brahma was the one to do it.

Building the world

Some say that Brahma the creator then transformed into many different bodies and shed them as a snake sheds its skin. The discarded bodies became essential parts of the new world, such as night and day, gods and ancestors who carried the spirit of goodness, the dark forces of the demons, and humankind.

The lotus-eyed boar prized out Earth from the regions of Hell.

Others say that Brahma turned into a great boar with eyes like a lotus in full bloom. The boar pierced the regions of hell with his long, curved tusks, and prized out the Earth that was lying there, waiting to be reformed.

The boar laid the Earth gently over the ocean, and then smoothed its surface level in some places and piled up mountains in others. He set the rivers in their courses, and divided the Universe into sky, continents, and the underworld.

This is just one beginning of one universe. In an endless stream of time and space, universes are created and disappear. Each time, Vishnu recreates himself in a different form to make sure that the new creations take place, and Brahma rises again from a fresh lotus blossom, and a new universe is born.

CONNECTIONS
• The Aztecs had a similar belief in a constant cycle of worlds being created, destroyed, and new worlds being created again.
• Ananta the serpent may have been inspired by the king cobra, which lives deep in the jungles of India, often near water. A serpent also plays an important part in the Judeo-Christian story of Adam and Eve—but instead of being a protector, it is a wicked, lowly creature who tempts Eve to disobey her god.
• Some experts see parallels between the gods of India and those of ancient Greece, Egypt, and Mesopotamia. Hindu myths were written in Sanskrit, a language similar to ancient Greek, and the lesser gods have similar roles on Earth to Zeus and the Olympian gods of ancient Greece.

The lotus flower helped Brahma in his search inside himself to find out why he was there. Hindu belief is that knowledge, wisdom and creativity only come through people seaching inside themselves.

The Giant Who Made the World

Ancient Chinese myths dealt mostly with everyday life, rather than the mysteries of creation. The story of Pan Gu came later, around the fourth century AD, to explain the life forces of yin and yang that were core to most Taoist beliefs.

*The Tao
gives birth to the One.
The One gives birth to the Two.
The Two
give birth to the Three—
the Three give birth to every living thing.
All things are held in yin and carry yang,
and they are held together in the Ch'i of teeming energy.*

Tao, the One, the Path, came from emptiness. There was neither dark nor light, form nor shape—only emptiness and sameness. From Tao came the infinite, perfect whole of the cosmos, in the shape of a hen's egg. A sigh came from within the egg—it was Ch'i, the Original Breath, which enabled the Three to be born— the opposites, Yin and Yang, and the creator god, Pan Gu.

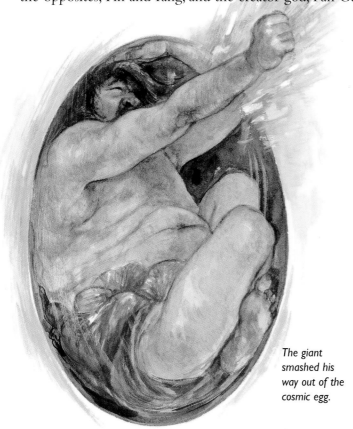

The giant smashed his way out of the cosmic egg.

Pan Gu lay inside the egg in a deep slumber for 18,000 years. As he slept, he grew until he was of the most gigantic proportions. When he awoke, he was cramped inside the cosmic egg, enclosed by impenetrable darkness that was without shape or form. Yin and Yang were there all around him, but they were joined, still and motionless. Their power was trapped.

Pan Gu drew himself up to his full height. He summoned all his energy, drew one mighty arm back and smashed it against the world that enclosed him. The shell of the egg cracked open. There was an explosion of energy like a bolt of electricity as Yin and Yang separated, the positive force of one striking against the negative energy of the other. Yang rose to be light and sky, while Yin consolidated into heavy earth and moisture. The Universe of Ten Thousand Things burst into being.

Gargantuan effort

Pan Gu needed to make more space between the Heavens and the Earth, between Yin and Yang. He planted his feet firmly astride on the ground and braced his shoulders. Each day, he pushed to ease the gap a fraction wider. Each day, the sky rose by 10 feet, and the foundations of the Earth deepened by 10 feet.

The giant had to grow at the same rate to keep in touch. At the same time, he had to carve the foundations of the world with his giant hammer and chisel, drawing on equal proportions of Yin and Yang in everything that he made.

It took another 18,000 years to reach the right distance between Heaven and Earth, and for Earth to be formed. At the end, Pan Gu was 28,000 miles tall and propped up the Heavens like an immense pillar. He had perspired heavily as he worked, and sometimes wept with the effort. His sweat and tears fell as rain upon the

Earth. Sometimes, he was happy—and then the weather was gentle and calm. Sometimes, though, he felt tired and lonely, depressed at the enormity of his task. Then, he grew angry. Storm clouds gathered, and bad weather raged through the Earth and skies.

The death of a weary giant

By the time his work was finished, Pan Gu was exhausted. Besides, he felt that the sky could support itself by now. He was so weakened by his great age and his labors, that his body sank to Earth in a crumpled heap. The giant was dying. But as his body began to disintegrate, marvelous changes took place. The wind and clouds of the future floated from Pan Gu's dying breath, his last words of agony became thunder, the sun, and the moon came from his eyes. The limbs of the huge, broken body formed the edges of the world—north, south, east, and west, and his blood flowed and gathered as lakes, seas, and rivers. From Pan Gu's flesh came soil in which plants could grow, while bones and teeth became solid rock and the veins of metals that run through them. Bone marrow turned into priceless gems.

Trees, grass, and flowering plants sprang from the hair on Pan Gu's head, while his fine body hair rose into the

The mighty giant, Pan Gu, chiseled and hammered the foundations of the Earth with his huge tools.

skies to form stars. Bugs overran the giant's decomposing body—and these turned into people.

It was very clear that humans were rather insignificant in the order of things, at least against the magnificence of the newly created world!

CONNECTIONS

• This story explains the ideas of Taoism, an ancient Chinese philosophy (way of thinking). The word "Tao" means "the right way"—that is, the right way of living, in harmony with the natural world. A similar theme occurs in Japanese mythology.

• Chinese Taoists believe that energy and life are sparked by the interaction of positive and negative forces, yin and yang. Each of these opposing forces contains the seed of the other; both forces are present in every living thing. Perfection and harmony are achieved when there is a balance of equal parts of yin and yang.

Chinese landscape paintings traditionally feature tiny human figures against magnificent terrains. The minor role of humans in the big picture echoes their lowly entrance into the world from Pan Gu's body bugs.

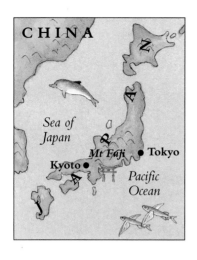

CHINA
Sea of Japan
Mt Fuji • Tokyo
Kyoto •
Pacific Ocean

Trials of Love

There are clues in this myth about how people were expected to behave in the Yamato court of seventh-century Japan, when the story was written. The story incorporates beliefs of the Shinto religion, the native religion of ancient Japan. The existence of spirits in living and inanimate objects, the balancing of opposites, and the importance of ritual behavior are key Shinto beliefs.

Something in the lifeless dark slowly gathered to a point at which the ethereal heavens separated from the solid Earth. As yet, there was no life force, no light, and absolutely nothing that a name could be put to. Various spirits appeared out of nothing, began the work of creation, and then they vanished again. The last two spirits, however, were to give birth to the islands of Japan.

He was called Izanagi, The Man Who Invites, and she was Izanami, The Woman Who Invites. Together they went to the Floating Bridge of Heaven, carrying a jewel-studded spear. They stood on the bridge and looked down at the ocean far beneath them. They lowered the spear into the seas and stirred, the woman's calm waters mixing with the man's rough waves. When Izanagi lifted the spear, salt water dripped from its tip and became an island on the ocean surface. He planted the spear into the land and around it built the

Giving birth to her last child, the spirit of fire, killed Izanami.

Palace of the Heavenly Pillar. Izanagi and Izanami then made this their home.

Children of love

One day, they played a game. Izanagi went around the heavenly pillar in one direction, and Izanami went around it the other way. They bumped into each other, and she immediately exclaimed, "Oh, what a handsome man!"

He replied, "And you are a beautiful woman. But as the man, I should have spoken first. We will have bad luck because you spoke first."

True enough, their firstborn child was crippled at birth. They decided to try the pillar game again, only this time, Izanagi, The Man Who Invites, was quick to get his compliment in first.

"Oh, what a beautiful woman," he exclaimed, and Izanami responded, "What a handsome man!"

They had many children after that, and each child was perfect. All of them turned into creator spirits, who shaped the elements of the world—the rivers, the mountains, the seasons, and winds, trees, and plants. They lived in the things that they had made forever after.

Life and death

The last child born to Izanagi and Izanami was the spirit of fire. When the spirit was born, it burned its mother so badly burned that she died and had to go to the Land of the Night. Izanagi was distraught. He followed his beloved Izanami, hoping to entice her back to the Land of the Living.

When he found her, he reeled back in horror and disbelief, for his wife had already eaten the food of the dead. Her once-beautiful body was disintegrating; the perfect skin was peeling from her putrefying flesh—decomposition had set in. Izanagi's agony at seeing her was the beginning of suffering in the world.

Izanagi and Izanami walked around the pillar, each delighting in the other's beauty.

Now for a man to see a woman in such a state broke the strictest of taboos. Izanami was mortified and angry. She banished her husband and ordered armies of demons to chase him. Izanagi fled for his life. He reached the entrance to the Land of the Night and blocked it with an enormous rock that would take 10,000 normal people to move. This made his deceased wife even angrier.

"For doing that," she shrieked, "I will destroy 1,000 of the people on your land every day."

"Well, in that case," he retorted, "I will make women suffer forever from childbirth. Every day, 1,500 of them will bear a child."

And so the cycle of life and death began. ▶

CONNECTIONS

• Izanagi and Izanami's delight in the gentle climate and beautiful plants is reflected in many Japanese traditions, from myths, to delicate paintings and beautiful gardens.
• As in China, the different dynasties that ruled Japan through the ages adapted their myths to glorify their own ancestors and to teach people how to behave. It was correct, for example, in Japanese society for the man to have the first word, and absolutely taboo for a man to see a woman in a less than perfect state.

Temple gardens in Japan are miniature versions of natural landscapes. Just like the myths of ancient Japan, they echo the harmony and balance found in Nature. It is said that the spirits described in Japan's oldest stories still live within animals and birds, in cherry blossoms and maple trees, in still lakes and running waters, and even in inanimate objects, such as rocks and minerals.

Trials of Love

Izanagi fathers new gods

After the first man spirit, Izanagi, had visited the Land of the Night and been surrounded by putrefying bodies, he could not wait to rid himself of the smell.
He stopped at the first river he came to, threw off his clothes, and plunged into the water. Behind him, his robe, sash, and all his jewels magically transformed themselves into spirits. More spirits flew from the spray as Izanagi's body cut through the water, and still more from the ripples that streamed behind his body.

The greatest of the newborn spirits was Amaterasu, who emerged when Izanagi bathed his left eye. She was called the Heaven Shining Great August Spirit, and was goddess of the sun. The moon god, Tsukiyomi—His August Moon Night Possessor—was born from Izanagi's right eye. Then Susano, the swift, brave, and impetuous storm god, was born as he washed his nose.

The storm god gathers strength

Right from the start, stormy Susano was at odds with the gentle, wise, and good Amaterasu. His dark clouds constantly warred against her tranquil radiance. His raging tornadoes flooded the fields and uprooted the crops she had introduced; his hurricanes pounded the landscape and turned trees upside down.

Eventually, Amaterasu became so upset by the endless disturbance, that she retreated deep into a remote cave, high up in the mountains. Immediately, endless night fell on the Earth like a cloak of darkness, and the twilight powers of evil reigned unchecked.

Something had to be done to bring Amaterasu out to shine once more. Eight million starlike—and very determined—spirits gathered on the Plain of Heaven, which lay beneath the cave's entrance. They planted hundreds of trees in front of the cave and hung jewels on every branch and twig. They lit bonfires so that the jewels caught the fire and threw it out into the darkness in twinkling shafts of ruby, emerald and diamond-white light. A thousand songbirds flew in to perch on the trees, and they filled the still night air with their sweet melodies.

The dancing spirits

Even so, Amaterasu, the goddess of the sun, was not tempted from her cave. Then, one spirit began to dance. She danced so wildly, leaping and twirling madly in the

The storm god, Susano, brought tornadoes and hurricanes to damage the Earth.

The first people to settle on the islands of Japan probably came from mainland Asia, in search of less harsh and barren land, and Japan became famous for its beautiful gardens. The awareness of Nature in Japanese mythology has parallels in Chinese philosophy.

CONNECTIONS

• Amaterasu was believed to be the ancestress of the Japanese imperial dynasties. Japan is sometimes known as "The Empire of the Sun," in honor of the radiant Amaterasu, and its national flag bears the sun as its emblem. After the Second World War, the Japanese emperor Hirohito renounced his divine descent from Amaterasu.
• Bathing and cleansing take on a ritualistic importance in Japan. It was Izanagi's top priority to jump into the stream and get clean after his encounter with the rotting body of his wife in the Land of the Night.

jewel-glinting darkness, that the other spirits became completely carried away, and cheered and entreated her to dance and dance again.

"More, more," they all cried, leaping about.

Inside her cave, Amaterasu heard the commotion and just could not resist peeping outside to see what was going on. The spirits acted immediately. They held a mirror before Amaterasu's face, so that the goddess could see her own reflection. Now, Amaterasu had never seen a mirror before.

"Look," they challenged, "you have a rival. There is someone who shines more brightly than you out here."

Gleaming jewels and singing songbirds were used to try to tempt Amaterasu, the goddess of the sun, out from her cave.

Triumph of the sun

The thought of a superior rival was quite intolerable to Amaterasu. She emerged at once from the dark cave. At once, a bright light and a warmth far greater than that from a thousand bonfires filled the world. Amaterasu stayed to give light to the Earth, disappearing only in the evenings, when night fell softly upon the planet.

Amaterasu was now the supreme deity. From her were descended all of the imperial families of Japan.

Animal Magic

The Dayak people live along rivers in the rain forests of Borneo. Mangrove swamps stretch from the coasts to the dense jungle inland, in one of the wettest regions on Earth. Rivers are rich in fish, and the forests teem with wild pigs, deer, bears, snakes, and a multitude of insects. The gods and spirits are part of every living thing.

Long, long ago, there was no Earth or sea, no mangrove swamps or jungle. Out of the void of the Heavens, a shape loomed—a monstrous spider that abseiled down on a silken rope that played out from its abdomen. The spider came to a halt and spun a web, until there was a floating, billowing net hanging in the emptiness.

A piece of coral, pink-red and hard as bone, plummeted through the Heavens like a meteorite. It hit the center of the giant hammock web and bounced—boing, boing, boing—as if on a giant trampoline. When it finally came to a rest, the coral broadened into a flat, round pancake shape, making a vast floor of solid rock under the skies.

A slug and a snail slowly somersaulted through the sky, and landed—splat—on the ground. Their slimy bodies spread over the coral land, turning into thick brown mud, like the mud dumped by sluggish rivers when they reach the sea.

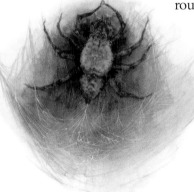

The monstrous spider spun a web like a giant trampoline.

Next, a young tree parachuted down from Space. It anchored its roots in the snail-and-slug mud, and flourished. The tree bore many fruits, which ripened in the steamy atmosphere and burst, scattering their seeds on the ground. The rain forest was born.

High in the Heavens, a land crab of monstrous proportions lurched clumsily toward Earth. It landed on its eight horny legs, pincers waving, and started dashing around. Dancing and scurrying in its sideways manner, the land crab scooped up some soil from beneath the rain forest trees and rearranged it into hills. It gouged valleys and basins in the sticky mud, and scooped up mounds to make mountains.

When the crab had finished its work, rain fell. The river courses and cavities in the Earth filled with water. Tender green shoots of myriad plants—bamboo, thorny sago palm, sweet potato, and rubber—miraculously appeared, pushing up through the ground.

Craftworking spirits

A pair of heavenly spirits arrived on the newly-made Earth and sat down to rest in the jungle. They hacked a branch from a tree and whittled the wood into shapes. The male spirit made the hilt of a sword, and the

CONNECTIONS
• The Dayak people live very close to Nature, like the Native American peoples. They believe that spirits live in every living thing, and do not believe that humans are superior to animals and plants. They watch how plants and animals behave for clues as to what the gods want, and believe that animals have thoughts and feelings just like those of humans. When they are hunting, they speak quietly or in codes, so that the animals don't discover their plans.

Several Dayak families may live in the village longhouse. They have separate living spaces, but there is a central communal area where they may meet, often to hear traditional stories. The stories may be sung or chanted by a cloaked bard (poet).

A pair of carved wooden heads appeared in the ghostly loom, but they had no bodies and were unable to move.

female spirit made a loom for weaving. When they had finished and were admiring their work, the male spirit accidentally dropped the sword hilt into the loom. The two objects interacted in a very strange way: the loom gave birth to two human heads, perfectly carved in wood! The heads had no bodies, however, and appeared lifeless. The male and female spirits found their offspring so dull that they returned to Heaven.

Humans, step-by-step

The heads managed to have two children of their own, who were actually able to move. Unfortunately, each one had only a head, a neck, and a bottom. It didn't stop them having their own children, though, and these two children were born with arms. In fact, their arms grew so long that they reached the sky.

These last two children were called Amei Awi and Burun Une, and they became the Dayak gods of agriculture. Amei Awi made a longhouse from bamboo. He collected shavings of bark from trees and scattered them around the house. The woodchips transformed

into chickens, dogs, and pigs. Amei Awi and Burun Une had twelve children of their own. Four of them became the spirits of the four quarters of the moon; the other eight were human—with full sets of working limbs.

When they were old enough, the humans were ordered by their parents to climb a particular mountain. The strongest climbed to the top. They became the ancestors of all slaves, because they did most work. Some people just climbed half way up and chose to stop. They became the first free people who looked after their own lives. Two humans didn't bother to climb anywhere—they just stayed at the bottom of the mountain, sitting and talking. If they wanted anything done, they told someone else to do it for them. These were the ancestors of all chiefs and kings.

As for Amei Awi and Burun Une, their work on Earth was finished. They went below ground—from where they control the rice harvest and wild plants to this very day.

Hawaii
Pacific Ocean
Tonga Marquesa Is.
Fiji Cook Is.
AUSTRALIA
NEW ZEALAND
Mangaia people

The Cosmic Coconut

For the Mangaia people of the Cook Islands of Polynesia, coconuts have long been a staple plant of survival. They remain an important crop even today. Coconuts provide food, drinks, and also fiber—which can be made into matting and ropes—all in one handy package.

A coconut hurtles from the crown of a palm tree far above and hits the sand with a thud. It lies on the beach, an oval husk bigger than a football. The local people crack open the husk to reveal the leathery-skinned kernel. The thin layer beneath is tough and fibrous, and surrounds a thickness of crunchy white flesh that is full of nutritious oils. Deeper still is a sweet, refreshing drink of coconut milk.

Living in the Silent Land

The Universe itself is like a giant coconut shell. Inside is the place called Avaiki. At the bottom of the inner world of Avaiki lies the Silent Land. At the beginning of time, a female demon lived there. She was called Vari'-ma-te-akere, which means "The Very Beginning." It was very cramped in the narrow space of the Silent Land, and Vari' had to sit hunched up, her knees pressed against her chin. Being unable to move was very boring. Vari' decided to make life more exciting by having many children. Her offspring would be the builders of the world.

Vatea was half-fish, half-human.

Children of the new world

Vari' tore a lump of flesh from one side of her body, and made the first male, whom she called Vatea. He was a very odd creature. One side of him looked like a man, with half a human head, an arm, and a leg. The other half was like a porpoise, with a fin instead of an arm, and a tail instead of a leg. His eyes radiated light, but one was a human eye, the other like a porpoise eye. One eye became the sun, the other became the moon. It was impossible to see both eyes at the same time. After all, when the sun is visible to the outside world, the moon is not, for it is shining in the inner world of Avaiki.

Vari' made more children from her body, and each one of them had a special place in the cosmic coconut. Vatea's land was filled with the brilliant light of the noonday sun. As firstborn son and father of all gods, he lived at the top, just beneath a tiny crack that opened to the world of the mortals beyond. He was to become lord of the oceans and would be worshiped by all mortals.

Vari''s second child was another fishy character called Tinirau. He was dispatched to the land called the Sacred Isle. Here, Tinirau made huge ponds and stocked them with all kinds of fish—for he was to be lord of all the finned creatures of the sea. Tango, who was master of the tropical forests, lived in the luscious Land of the Red Parrot Feathers, while Tumu teanaoa, also known as Echo,

CONNECTIONS

• The idea of the Universe as a coconut may seem strange to people of temperate lands. It is not so different from imagining the Universe as an egg (in China), which also represents birth and growth, and contains all the elements we need for survival.

• Cook Islanders and the Maoris are from the same Polynesian stock and have similar myths. Papa, the Earth mother of this story, for example, reappears in a different guise in Maori myth.

Coconuts—used for food and soap—are the fruits of the coconut palm. They narrow at the point where they meet the stem that attaches them to the tree. This is like the narrow space in the cosmic coconut where Vari' lived.

lived among the Hollow Grey Rocks, from which the rocky foundations of the Earth were to be dragged.

The god Raka dwelt in the coconut milk land that was called Deep Ocean. Vari' presented him with a big basket that contained the winds of the world—squalls and hurricanes, and gentle sea breezes.

Their sandy-haired son, Tangaroa, was the ancestor of all red things, such as the chestnut tree and the red yam, and of blond-haired children. Black-haired Rongo was father of everything else, and of dark-haired children.

Vatea lowered a tasty morsel of coconut down a pothole, and the beautiful Papa reached out her hand to grasp it.

she vanished as soon as he awoke. Perhaps she dwelt in one of the kingdoms beneath, he wondered. He peered down the deep potholes that peppered the floor of his land. "Maybe if I lower some tasty morsels of coconut," he thought, "they will act like bait, and I will catch my beautiful fish."

He did this, and when he hauled up a chunk he noticed that it had been nibbled.

Vatea lowered more pieces and kept watch. Soon he saw a graceful hand reach out. It belonged to Papa, the foundation, the future Earth. Vatea had found the love of his life. They had twin children who created many plants for the Mangaian world, and they taught mortals how to farm.

But it was the last-born child who was Vari''s favorite. She was given the name Tu-metua, which means "stick-by-the-parent." Tu-metua lived with her mother in the Silent Land. The two never said a word to each other, but they expressed their emotions and feelings with silent smiles and eyes that spoke volumes.

Bribery by coconut

At the opposite end of the coconut realm, Vatea, the father of all gods, was not sleeping well. His dreams were haunted by a most beautiful woman, but

The birth of an island

Now at the top of a real coconut are three "eyes." From one of them, the shoot of a new coconut palm appears. In the cosmic coconut, this opening was where the island of Mangaia—the center of the world—was pulled from. Contained within it were all the elements that made up the different realms of Avaiki.

Real men and women lived on Mangaia, while those from other islands were believed to be evil spirits posing as humans. When the British explorer, Captain James Cook, discovered the islands in 1773, the Mangaian people decided that he must have come from Vatea's bright land by breaking through the shell of the coconut.

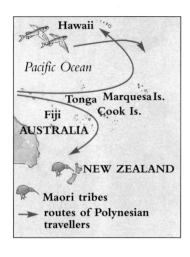

Hawaii
Pacific Ocean
Tonga   Marquesa Is.
Fiji   Cook Is.
AUSTRALIA

NEW ZEALAND

Maori tribes
routes of Polynesian
travellers

Violent Beginnings

The Maori people of New Zealand originally came from the islands of Polynesia in the Pacific Ocean. There are links between their myths and those of other Polynesian peoples. The distances that separated the Pacific peoples, and different landscapes and lifestyles, led to local variations in myths. A common theme is that creation can begin only if opposites, such as Earth and sky, are separated.

There was no glimmer of dawn, no clearness, no light. In the primeval waste of water and darkness, Io, the cosmic soul, was born in a breath. In Io were all the ingredients of the world to come. First came Papa and Rangi, Earth mother and sky father. They were like twins joined at birth, so close was their embrace. There was no space for light, life itself was trapped. Papa and Rangi's children became extremely frustrated.

"Why is it everywhere dark?" they said. "We can't create the world." Warlike Tu spoke up. "We must kill Papa and Rangi, and force them apart."

Kindly Tane proposed a less violent solution. "Let's part them gently, without pain. Rangi, our sky father, will rise far above us. He will become a stranger, but Papa will rest beneath our feet, and be close to us, just as a mother should be."

Tane was a strong, gentle spirit, maker of the plants and creatures of the forests.

The parting of the parents

All the brothers and sisters agreed on this plan—apart from Tawhiri, spirit of winds and storms. He worried that a world of light and life would be too beautiful, too perfect. There might be no place for the storms and dark clouds of his kingdom, and he would become powerless.

Nevertheless, the other gods set about their task. Each one of them tried pulling and pushing in every direction, in their attempts to separate Papa and Rangi.

Even Tane, the strong, gentle forest god, failed at first. Then he tried a headstand. He planted his enormous head on Papa, the Earth, bent his legs, and—straining with every muscle and sinew in the trunk of his body—he forced his feet up against Rangi.

A chilling cry pierced the atmosphere. "Why are you tearing us apart? How can you do this to your parents?"

Tane pushed even more strongly, and with a final thrust, Heaven and Earth split apart. Immediately, light flooded into the space between, and myriad little creatures spilled out. They were the first people and animals, who up to now had been trapped in the entwined bodies of Papa and Rangi.

CONNECTIONS

• The peoples of Polynesia migrated thousands of miles across the Pacific Ocean, settling new lands separated by vast tracts of sea. Despite a time scale of 3,000 years, links in their oral traditions can still be traced. For the Maori people of New Zealand, Io is the Supreme Being; the same word in Hawaiian means "truth," and in the Cook Islands, it means "god."

• Papa and Rangi are torn apart in this story. Other creation myths also feature a destruction that creates new things. Aztec worlds were created from conflict between gods who were opposites, like the Chinese forces of yin and yang.

It was in more simple versions of this carved wooden canoe that the Maori people paddled over 3,000 miles of ocean before they arrived in New Zealand. The first settlers were established over 700 years before the first Europeans arrived in the 1600s. They probably came from the Polynesian Marquesa Islands.

Life in a new land

The young gods could now begin work. Tane brought day and night, and clothed the naked Earth with grasses, ferns, and forests. He released animals into the new land: the brush-tailed possum, the flightless kiwi birds, and the kakapo parrot. Over his father in the sky, he draped a star-spangled cloak that was edged with the red glow of sunrise and sunset. The Earth took shape, as the gods made the mountains, volcanoes, the flowing rivers, and steaming geysers.

Tawhiri, the storm god, was furious that chaos had been destroyed. He attacked Earth with fierce rains and screaming winds. Lofty pine trees, silver-barked beeches and the crimson-flowered Pohutukawa trees were uprooted in floods. Tawhiri turned on Tangaroa, the sea god, and whipped up tidal waves of destruction. Tangaroa took refuge in the deep seas. Some of his offspring stayed with him and became fish, but others fled to the land and became lizards and other reptiles.

Tu, the warrior, was the only god who stood up to the storm god and eventually stilled him. But Tu deeply resented the fact that none of his brothers and sisters had helped him. They were much too busy reproducing, while Tu was doing all the work. In fact, they had so many offspring that Tu felt quite threatened. So he decided to wage war on them, too, and destroy their creations. He even attacked the gentle Haumia, god of foods that grow in the wild, and Rongo, creator of cultivated foods, and tore up the world's plants. Just in time, he realized that he was destroying his own food supply, so to insure that life on Earth could continue, Tu gave each of the gods special chants so that they could create new generations of children.

As for the storm god Tawhiri, you can see his offspring today, forever interfering on land and at sea. They are the squalls and whirlwinds, gloomy fogs, and clouds that burst into thunder, or carry the sun's ruby glow.

There had been so many battles among Papa and Rangi's children that the sea rose and overwhelmed great tracts of land—which may explain why the Pacific Ocean is there today, scattered with islands of firm ground.

The fierce warrior, Tu, finally wore out Tawhiri's wind armies. Because none of the other gods would fight with him, he wreaked his revenge.

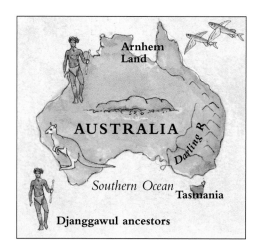

Dreaming

The Dreamtime of the Australian Aborigines is the source of all life. There are different versions of the tale, but all share the belief that ancestral spirits shaped the world at the beginning of time. The adventures of the Ancestors are relived today in ceremonies, dance, songs, and paintings. The continent is an intricate web of sacred trails.

The 12-year-old boy watched and learned from his father as they followed the trail. The tiniest snapped twig, displaced fragment of rock, or faint trace of a foot track, which would be invisible to anyone else but a member of the same tribe, marked their way. Father and son were following in the steps of the ancestral spirits, and generations of their tribe before them. From time to time on their journey they saw kangaroos, emus, and possums. The flat, sandy plains were pockmarked with stunted salt bushes and trees. Otherwise, to the untrained eye at least, the sunburned landscape stretched to far-off horizons.

After three days and nights crossing the sand dunes and the dry, sparse tropical woodland, they came to the billabong, the still water of the creek ringed by rustling tamarisk trees. In the shade, beneath an overhang, they found figures painted on the rockface in tan, black, and white.

The beginning of all things

"This, my son," explained the older man, "is a sacred place, made by the Ancestors, who made us and all things. They are sleeping here, now, in these trees, in the rock and the water.

"The time when the Ancestors made the world was the Dreamtime. The Dreamtime still is, it is now forever, and has always been. It is life itself, and the source of all life." The man and the boy squatted by

The Ancestors arose from their slumber beneath the Earth and pushed through the ground—as people, snakes, plants, kangaroos, and mixtures of all of these.

the water hole. They picked the thorns from their bare feet, and sated their thirst from the still waters. They looked out over the vastness of plain and twiggy salt bushes simmering still beneath the setting sun. The reds and golds of the plain deepened, the shadows cast by the rocks and trees lengthened. Then darkness fell, suddenly, as if a blanket had been dropped over the land.

"Before the Dreamtime," continued the older man, "there was a flat, barren plain and it was always dark. There were no trees, or water holes, kangaroos, or snakes. There was no life at all, and no death, either."

The first stars pierced the velvet blackness of the night sky. "Before the beginning," the father explained, "the stars, the moon, and the sun were sleeping beneath the plain. There was no light at all.

"Many Ancestors slept beneath the plain. The time came, though, when they all woke up and thrust through the Earth's crust. Some of them looked a bit like us, others were giant kangaroos or snakes, and some were mixtures of animals and plants all in one body.

The journey of the Ancestors

"Djanggawul and his two sisters were the ancestral spirits of our people," the father continued. "They looked a bit like you and me. They began their journey in the Island of the Dead, over the seas far to the northeast. They set off in a bark canoe and paddled west over the turquoise tropical seas, guided by the sun as it traveled through the sky. Finally, they reached the dunes and mangrove swamps of our land."

The older man looked at his digging stick. "It's thanks to them that we can drink," he said. "They had digging sticks, too. Only theirs were special and sacred. As they strode over the burning, stinging sand, they'd stop sometimes, and plunge their sticks into the earth. Fresh water sprang from the holes and made many water holes like this one. Sometimes, when they dug their sticks into the ground, living trees grew.

Some of the Ancestors used their digging sticks to create water holes.

The father told how, as they journeyed through the land, Djanggawul and his sisters gave names to places and plants, animals and fish; to bandicoots, possums, and goannas, black cockatoos and geese, and flying foxes. Sometimes they met other ancestral beings on walkabout, and exchanged gifts with them. From time to time they stopped to rest and place dreams, which they called Dreamings, and make their sacred places.

"The Djanggawul ancestors peopled the land with their children, who were the first of our tribe," the father explained. "Before they moved on, they made sure the people knew how to survive, where to dig for witchetty bugs, and how to find food. That's what I am teaching you, and that's how I learned from my father how to hold our culture and our land sacred forever."

"Never forget what I have told you," he said. "The time will come when you will have children, and then you will pass the knowledge down to them."

Dreaming inside and outside

The Ancestors had created the world and people. So they went back to sleep, some back beneath the Earth, others became rocks and trees. Their Dreamings are all around us and inside us, too. They were a long time ago, but they are also now and forever.

CONNECTIONS

- The continuing spiritual presence in all things, and the viewing of humans and animals as equals, with their lives closely intertwined, is common to many living tribal myths, including those of the Dayak of Borneo and the Native Americans.
- The Aborigines believe that Dreamtime exists simultaneously (at the same time) with the present, the here and now. People slip into Dreamtime when they fall asleep. Long ago, there was only sleep; then came the split that separated sleeping and waking.

A billabong, or creek, can be like an oasis in the vast expanses of Australian bush and desert. For the Aborigines, many billabongs are sacred places that were made by the ancestral spirits, places where the spirits still live today.

Glossary

aborigines Original or early inhabitants of a land, who were there before invading powers introduced new settlers.

Amaterasu Japanese sun goddess.

Amei Awi Dayak god of agriculture.

Ananta In Hindu myth, the serpent that contains the elements of all living things.

ancestors Long-dead members of a family, such as great-great grandparents, from whom generations that are living are descended.

Ancestors, the Creator gods of the aboriginal people of Australia.

Anu Mesopotamian sky god.

Aphrodite Greek goddess of love.

Apsu Mesopotamian creator god of freshwater, husband of saltwater Tiamat.

Ask First man, in Nordic mythology.

Atum First of ancient Egyptian creator gods.

Atunda Servant of Yoruba creator god, Orisa-nla, who destroyed his master and so enabled spirits—or orishas—to be created.

Audhumla First animal (a cow) to be created, in Nordic mythology.

Avaiki Inner world of the coconut-like universe in mythology of the Mangaian people (Cook Islands).

Aztec Central American people who lived in northern and central Mexico. The empire they built up was at its most powerful between AD 1350 and AD 1520.

Bestla Nordic giantess, daughter of Ymir, wife of Bor, and mother of Odin, Vili, and Ve.

Bible Holy book of the Jewish and Christian faiths.

Bor Nordic god, son of Buri, and father of Odin, Vili, and Ve.

Brahma Hindu creator god.

Buri Creator deity of Nordic mythology, son of Ymir, the frost giant.

Burun Une Dayak god of agriculture.

Chalchiuhtlicue Aztec goddess of streams and lakes.

chaos State of complete disorder.

Chaos Greek god who predated order and life on Earth.

Ch'i The original breath that contained yin and yang, in Taoist belief.

civilization A society that has developed laws and education, and where many people have settled in towns.

cosmos The ordered whole of Earth and the Heavens.

culture A collective word for the beliefs, customs, language, and way of life that identify a particular people or civilization.

deity God or goddess.

divine Sacred or like a god.

Djanggawul Creator ancestors of Australian Aborigines, in particular, those from the northern region of Arnhem Land. *Djang* means sacred.

Dreamtime The continuing state of creation and being that is central to the beliefs of the Australian Aborigines.

Ea All-knowing Mesopotamian god, father of Marduk.

Embla First woman, in Nordic mythology.

Eros Greek god of desire.

Esaugetuh Emissee Master of Breath, who the Muskogees, or Creek Indians, believed breathed life into the world.

eternity For ever and ever.

Faro Water spirit and creator god of Bambara mythology.

Furies Avenging spirits in ancient Greek mythology.

Gaia Greek Earth mother, partner of Ouranos, the sky god.

Geb Ancient Egyptian Earth god, twin of sky goddess, Nut.

generation Refers to people who are born around the same time. You and your friends and brothers and sisters are one generation, your parents are another.

Hemera Greek goddess of day.

Izanagi and **Izanami** Creator spirits in Japanese mythology, also known as The Man Who Invites and The Woman Who Invites.

Koran Holy book of the Islamic faith.

Kronos Last-born Greek Titan, who killed his father, Ouranos, married Rhea, and became the father of Zeus and other Olympian gods.

legend Ancient story that has been handed down over the years, and which usually includes actual events and people.

Marduk Chief Babylonian god, who wrested power from the sea goddess Tiamat.

meditation Focussed, deep thinking, and questioning. In spiritual contexts, meditation is often done in a controlled, trancelike state.

migration Movement of people (or animals, birds) from one region to settle in another, either permanently, or at certain times of the year, in search of food.

Musso-Koroni First woman of Bambara mythology and long-suffering wife of Pemba, the evil wood spirit.

myth Story with supernatural beings such as spirits, gods, and monsters, which has been handed down through generations. Myths usually reflect the beliefs or customs of a society.

mythology Collected myths and beliefs of a society.

Nun Endless ocean that preceded Earth in ancient Egyptian mythology.

Nut Ancient Egyptian sky goddess, and the twin of Earth god, Geb.

Nyx Greek goddess of night.

Obtalala The orisha (spirit) of Yoruba mythology who built the Earth with the help of a white hen.

Odin Chief Nordic god, who breathed life into the first humans.

Old Man Creator god of the Native American Blackfoot tribe.

Olodumare All-seeing, all-knowing head orisha (spirit) of Yoruba mythology.

Olympian One of 12 Greek gods who lived on Mount Olympus and involved themselves in the affairs of humans.

Ometeotl Creator god of the Aztec people.

Orisa-nla The one who came at the beginning, according to the Yoruba people of West Africa.

orisha Spirit of Yoruba mythology, born from fragments of Orisa-nla.

Orunmilla Yoruba spirit of wisdom.

Ouranos Greek god of the sky, partner of Gaia, Earth mother.

Pan Gu Chinese creator god.

Papa Earth mother in Polynesian and Maori mythology.

Pemba Evil, power-hungry wood spirit of Bambara mythology.

primeval Describes the earliest age of the world.

primordial Describes things that existed before the world as we know it began.

Quetzalcoatl Aztec plumed serpent god of air, sun, water, and fertility.

Ra Ancient Egyptian sun god.

Rangi Sky father of Maori myth, partner of Earth mother, Papa.

Rhea A Titan, sister and wife of Kronos, who became the mother of Zeus and other Olympian gods.

ritual Often repeated set of actions, particularly as a part of religious ceremonies, as a way of communicating with the gods.

Shu Ancient Egyptian god of air.

sun One of the five worlds that the Aztecs believed was created and then destroyed.

Susano Japanese storm god.

Tane Maori god of plants and creatures of the forest.

Tao Origin of everything in Eastern mythology. Its literal meaning is "the Path" or "the right way" (of living in harmony with the natural world).

Tawhiri Storm and wind god of the Maori peoples.

Tefnut Ancient Egyptian rain goddess, mother of Geb and Nut.

Tezcatlipoca Ruler of the first new world in Aztec mythology.

Tiamat Mesopotamian creator god of the saltwaters, wife of freshwater Apsu.

Titans The 12 early Greek gods, offspring of the creator gods Gaia and Ouranos, who preceded the Olympian gods.

Tlaloc Aztec rain god.

tradition Habits, customs, and beliefs handed down through generations to become part of a people's identity.

tribe Group of people who share a common language and a simple way of life, such as one based on hunting and gathering for food.

Tu Maori warrior god.

Underworld The imaginary place beneath the Earth where the dead live.

Universe Earth, the Heavens and all that is in them.

Vari'-ma-te-akere Female demon in Mangaian (Cook Island) mythology, whose name means the beginning of everything.

Vatea First male, albeit half-man, half-fish, in the mythology of the Mangaian people.

Ve Key Nordic god, who granted humans speech, hearing, and sight.

Vili Senior Nordic god, who gave humans emotions and intelligence.

Vishnu Hindu god, who is within all universes, past and present.

yin and yang Positive and negative forces present in all things, which produce energy when they react against each other, and harmony when equally balanced.

Ymir Frost giant, the first creator god of Nordic mythology.

Xiuhtecuhtli (Ksew-tec-ewt-lee) Aztec god of fire.

Yo Sound at the very root of creation, in Bambara mythology.

Zeus Chief Olympian god in mythology of ancient Greece.

Index